STRENGTH IN THE STORM

STRENGTH IN THE STORM

CREATING CALM IN DIFFICULT TIMES

EKNATH EASWARAN

JAICO PUBLISHING HOUSE

Ahmedabad Bangalore Chennai
Delhi Hyderabad Kolkata Mumbai

Published by Jaico Publishing House
A-2 Jash Chambers, 7-A Sir Phirozshah Mehta Road
Fort, Mumbai - 400 001
jaicopub@jaicobooks.com
www.jaicobooks.com

Published in arrangement with
Nilgiri Press
P.O. Box 256
Tomales, California 94971, USA
www.easwaran.org

To be sold only in India, Bangladesh, Bhutan,
Pakistan, Nepal, Sri Lanka and the Maldives.

STRENGTH IN THE STORM
ISBN 81-7992-583-8

First Jaico Impression: 2006
Sixth Jaico Impression: 2013

Printed by
Repro India Limited, Mumbai

About This Book

By Christine Easwaran

This book is about coping with stress and anxiety – finding strength to meet the challenges and even the major crises that all of us face in everyday life.

I don't know anyone better qualified to make this presentation than Eknath Easwaran.* In our forty years together, I saw him weather crisis after crisis with love, compassion, and a clear-eyed faith in individual goodness that nothing could shake.

Of course, in saying this I cannot claim to be objective. My life has been linked with his since I first heard him speak in 1960, when he was at the peak of his academic career. A full professor of English at a major Indian university and known throughout India as a writer and lecturer, Easwaran had come to the University of California at Berkeley on the Fulbright exchange program. He was giving talks around the Bay Area on the spiritual heritage of India, and I was attracted to a series offered at a bookstore in San Francisco.

Although Easwaran drew large crowds on some of these occasions, that evening he had the intimate atmosphere he preferred

* *Eknath* is the family name; *Easwaran* is his given name.

all his life: a group of thirty to fifty people – about classroom size – in a setting personal enough for him to speak to each person heart to heart. These were not dry academic talks. To him, the world's spiritual traditions were not topics for philosophy or religion. They were living waters, practical resources for everyday living. And he was a gifted, inspired teacher. I saw at once that he had answers to questions I had been asking, and he had a burning desire to share his insights with all who would listen.

I quickly joined the small group of people who surrounded him at the various locations in the Bay Area where he was making friends and influencing lives. Eager to help him spread his message, we provided transportation, meeting places, fresh audiences, whatever was needed. Eventually someone suggested that he formalize his work, and the Blue Mountain Center of Meditation was established late in 1961.

From those small beginnings, mostly by word of mouth, Easwaran's reach grew. Books based on his talks began to appear, beginning with *Gandhi the Man* in 1972. By the time of his passing, in 1999, he had two dozen books translated into as many languages, and thousands of people around the world were following his Eight Point Program of passage meditation.

Meditation, however, requires systematic daily practice – a big hurdle in today's hurried world. For every individual who has learned to meditate along Easwaran's lines, there are thousands more whose lives have been changed simply by reading his books, drawing inspiration from his talks, or practicing some of the other skills in his Eight Point Program.

This book is intended for that much larger audience. Written with the authority of a gifted teacher of meditation, it doesn't assume that you want to meditate – at least not yet! Its purpose is to present other skills that anyone, even a child, can use to help face the challenges that life brings.

The key to facing these challenges, Easwaran maintains, is the mental state with which we meet them. All of us have inner resources for dealing creatively with what life throws at us. We simply have to learn how to release those resources – and that, he teaches, is essentially a matter of quieting the agitation in the mind. It's a simple idea, but one that goes deep: a truly calm mind can weather any storm.

Easwaran spent almost forty years teaching ordinary men and women how to keep their minds calm and kind in crisis, so that they become a center of strength for themselves and those around them. This is no quick fix; it's something we go on learning throughout our lives. Yet dramatic changes can come almost immediately, as I hope you'll discover for yourself when you try some of the simple techniques in this book.

You'll see three sections in each chapter:

- An introduction presenting Easwaran's timeless ideas in the light of problems and challenges that ordinary people face today.

- Easwaran's article – the main part of each chapter – follows my introduction. Each article presents a key idea, such as how living in the present helps keep the mind calm and secure.

These articles came from Easwaran's informal talks to close students, heightening the impression that he is speaking directly to us. Imagine yourself in his audience, listening to his stories, smiling at his gentle humor, sharing in his insights.

One person who comes up repeatedly in these articles is Easwaran's maternal grandmother, whom he later came to revere as his spiritual teacher. (The maternal lineage is important because the Eknath name is carried by the mother – part of an ancient matriarchal tradition in Kerala, South India, in which women have had land rights for centuries and are noted for their strength and independence.) "Granny," as Easwaran calls her, was his primary inspiration for translating spiritual wisdom into everyday life.

As you read these articles, you'll also find sidebars with illustrations from some of the people who tell us their difficulties and successes in applying Easwaran's teachings in the real world. (We've changed names and other details as necessary to protect privacy.) These examples help show the practical applications of what Easwaran is talking about.

- A workbook section concludes each chapter. These pages, based on years of experience in presenting Easwaran's teachings at retreats, are designed to help you get the most out of each article. A list of Key Ideas is followed by two pages of suggested activities – "Points to Practice"– and an inspirational passage of poetry or prose that speaks to the chapter's theme. This is the same kind of passage used in Easwaran's method of meditation, in which we absorb high ideals by filling our minds with them and then trying our best to live them out each day.

This combination – a real-life introduction, Easwaran's direct teaching, and a practical summary with daily experiments and the shared experiences of other students – is the same as what we follow in our retreats. It has been tested over and over with thousands of people who are applying his teachings in a busy life. Easwaran is a very practical teacher whose writing is packed with ideas. To understand him requires not just reading, but a bit of experimentation too.

It is my sincere hope that with this combination of timeless wisdom and practical illustration, you will discover the inner strength to weather any storm – the strength that Easwaran assures us is our birthright as human beings.

CHAPTER ONE

Strength in the Storm

Steadiness of mind is one of the most practical of skills. Nothing is more vital than learning to face turmoil with courage, confidence, and compassion.

Fortunately, we already possess these capacities. But we need a calm mind to draw on them. That is the practical importance of a calm mind.

Your Undiscovered Resources

Introduction by Christine Easwaran

Big or small, global or personal, stress and challenges are woven into the fabric of our days. Life takes us by surprise, pushing us to the limit and beyond.

Over the years, we have received thousands of letters from people telling us how Easwaran's teachings helped them face such times of turmoil. Some came from people we never met, who knew him only from his books; others came from friends who had come to our retreats. Their stories form a tapestry of modern life, from traffic irritations and angry encounters to brushes with death that remind us of what really matters.

One good friend, Chuck, wrote us about a particularly urgent surprise – the kind everyone dreads. It came just weeks after a long period of pain and stress from a hip replacement. While he was still recovering from the surgery, life decided to send him this:

Lynn and I were in town for dinner when the chest pains started. I'd had an incident a couple of months earlier that felt similar, and the diagnosis then was "digestive upset." I was reluctant to go into the emergency room again with the "same old problem."

"Hospital or home?" Lynn asked.

"I really don't know what to do," I said.

She took one look at me: "I do," she said. She pulled a fast right and headed for the hospital . . .

Stress isn't new, of course. All of us have our own stories to share. The problem with dramas like these is not so much that they come without warning, but that we are already burdened by anxieties about ongoing concerns beyond our control. When a crisis comes we're under stress already, simply from the load we carry in our daily lives: family responsibilities, tense relationships, money worries, work pressures, and those incessant, nagging fears about the state of our neighborhoods, our schools, the threat of terrorism, a world at war.

In the pages that follow, Easwaran makes a wise point we often forget: life will always be full of ups and downs, but we don't have to go up and down with it. We can't control what life sends us, but we can have a say in how we respond.

The secret is the mind. It is the mind that feels agitated, stressed, pressured, helpless, or anxious. And it is the mind that can learn to stay calm, resourceful, compassionate, and effective. Everything depends on our state of mind – the one thing in life we can do something about.

Within ourselves, Easwaran assures us, we already have the resources to meet and even thrive on challenges. We don't have to develop this capacity; everything we need is already present in the depths of our hearts. To draw on it, all we have to do is calm the mind so that its agitation doesn't get in the way. As we learn to do this, wonderful reserves of strength, love, wisdom, and creativity begin to flow into our lives.

In this chapter, Easwaran develops this idea and introduces a skill with truly limitless power to calm the mind. Other strategies follow in later chapters. With these simple techniques, thousands of people have learned not only to weather crises but to emerge from them a little stronger, a little wiser, a little more compassionate.

Chuck and the others we quote from in this book are people like these. They are Easwaran's students: ordinary men and women who have been practicing what he teaches and have written to tell us about their experiences. We've included two or three of these stories in every chapter – Chuck tells the conclusion of his on page 26.

Strength in the Storm

By Eknath Easwaran

My first encounter with an ocean storm came on my way to the U.S. on the Fulbright exchange program. I sailed from Bombay on an ancient P&O liner that had been in service before the first world war. There were no luxuries, but I enjoyed the trip because of the variety of passengers – from empire builders to scholars from the Far East – and the ever-changing beauty of the sea.

But July in the Arabian Sea is monsoon season, and three or four days out our little ship began to be tossed like a toy by winds and rain.

A storm is a great equalizer. All distinctions of class and color were swept away. Empire builders hung at the railings side by side with Asian academics, clutching identical brown bags. All of us cheered with relief when the weather passed and we were obliged to put in at Aden for repairs.

Sailing from Cherbourg to New York on HMS *Queen Mary* was an utterly different experience. The *Queen Mary* too was nearing retirement age. But she was fast, and positively luxurious by comparison with that P&O vessel. When we hit rough seas on the Atlantic, we sailed through majestically without a roll.

"Why aren't we being tossed about?" I asked an officer. "Is it because of the ship's size?"

"No," he said proudly, "it's the stabilizers. We installed them a couple of years ago. Now rough waters don't bother her at all."

I often recall those two journeys to illustrate one of the most important truths I have ever learned. Like a storm, life is a great equalizer. It does bring sunny days, but it is sure to bring storms as well. And regardless of class, color, status, birth, or wealth, some of us sail through surely while others flounder and even go under.

We can't control life, but we can control how we respond to life's challenges. The answer lies in stabilizing the mind.

Few human beings are born with the skill to weather storms and stress with grace. Yet everyone can learn. We can't control the weather outside, but we can control how we respond. Like the *Queen Mary,* we can install stabilizers – in the mind.

For it is in the mind that the storms of life really blow. What matters is not so much the turmoil outside us as the weather within. To a person with an agitated mind, something as minor as a rude driver can cause enough stress to ruin a day. By contrast I think of Mahatma Gandhi, who gave himself away when he confessed, "I love storms." Gandhi began life as a timid child, but he learned to keep his mind so steady that he could face tremendous crises with courage, compassion, wisdom, and even a sense of humor.

This steadiness of mind is one of the most practical of skills. Without it, no one can face the challenges of life without breaking. And life today is challenging to say the least. We live in the midst of conflicts – within ourselves, at home, in the community, even nationally and internationally. This is an age of conflict, which makes it an age of anxiety as well. Nothing is more vital than learning to face this turmoil with confidence and compassion.

Fortunately, we don't have to develop these capacities. We already have them. But we need a calm mind to draw on them. When the mind is agitated or confused, the deeper resources we require are simply locked up inside. That is the practical importance of a calm mind.

> We already have the capacity to deal with challenges. But we need a calm mind to draw on the resources locked up within.

So how do we calm the mind? One very powerful way is so simple that everyone can learn it easily, right now, even a child: the repetition of a mantram, or "prayer word" as it is called in some circles in the West. (*See sidebar on the next page.*)

You can think of the mantram as a handrail for the mind. It gives you something to hold on to, so that you can steady yourself in confusing circumstances until your thoughts become clear.

You can think of repeating the mantram as calling God collect – or, if you prefer, as an emergency call to your highest self.

Either way, repeating the mantram is an appeal for resources that are always present but seem invisible in times of trouble. "This is beyond me," we are saying. "I need strength I can't find – I can't even pay for this call. Please send help, and pick up the bill too."

The mantram is a tool for calming the mind that anyone can learn and use at any time.

What Is a Mantram?

What is a mantram? How can it help you? How does it work?

The term *mantram* (or *mantra*) stands for a word or short phrase that you can repeat silently to yourself to help you cope with stress. It has the power to calm and steady your mind whenever you need access to deeper reserves of strength or patience within you.

You may already be using stress reduction techniques such as counting to ten, taking a couple of deep breaths, or repeating a positive affirmation to yourself. All of these can help, but the mantram is just as quick, just as easy to use, and much more powerful. It combines immediate help with long-term benefits that, like a savings account, accumulate the more it's used.

This simple skill is thousands of years old. Saint Francis of Assisi, for example, repeated "My God and my all." Mahatma Gandhi used "Rama, Rama."

But you don't have to think of yourself as religious to use a mantram. It works for everyone, because it works directly on the mind. You'll see from the stories

If you're like me, at this point you may doubt that such a simple skill could do what I claim.

I doubted it, too, when my grandmother tried to tell me what the mantram can do. Granny was the wisest person I have ever known, and I loved her passionately, so I always took her advice seriously. But, after all, grannies don't know everything. "Granny,"

in this book how the mantram continues to help ordinary people face crises today.

How does the mantram help?

- It calms you down, whether you're facing a minor irritation or a major drama.
- It stops you from reacting too quickly and saying or doing something you may later regret.
- It halts rising anger, fear, and panic.
- It gives you a breathing space. Once you've got your mantram going, you'll find yourself in a much better state to choose your next move – and to choose it wisely.

The mantram works fast. If you start using it today, you'll probably feel the benefit of it the very next time you face a problem. But the more often you repeat the mantram, the deeper its benefits go.

For more on choosing and using a mantram, see the Points to Practice on page 32, right after this article. You'll find a fuller list of mantrams to choose from on the Web at www.easwaran.org/mantrams.

I protested, "that's just mindless repetition! What can repetition do?"

"Walking is just repetition too," she said. "One step after another, each one the same."

She had me there. But I still didn't believe her.

But life went on presenting challenges, and in college I encountered a really intimidating one: public speaking. I found the activity fascinating and took every opportunity to learn, but no matter how many times I stood before an audience and lived to tell the tale, I was always afraid that on the next occasion I would trip on my way to the podium or open my mouth and find that no words would come out.

When I confessed this fear to my granny, she had a very simple piece of advice: not to sit there going over my notes or trying to size up my audience, but to repeat the mantram to myself quietly while awaiting my turn.

I decided she didn't really understand. After all, she never had to give a speech! But because of my love for her, I promised to give it a try.

The next time I had to give a talk, I sat quietly repeating *Rama, Rama, Rama* over and over and over in my mind. Whenever my thoughts tried to blurt out "I'm afraid! I'm afraid!" instead, I would bring them back to "Rama, Rama" – adding to myself, every now and then, "I hope it works."

And the talk went well. With my mind calmer, the words came up right on cue.

I kept on practicing this little trick, and after a while I began to say, "*Rama, Rama, Rama* . . . I think it works!"

Today, after years of practice, I can assure you with complete confidence that I *know* it works. This is really the only way that trust in the mantram can come – through your own personal experience.

> Using a mantram is not just mechanical repetition. You learn to trust it by using it.

You can draw on the power of the mantram like this at any time, wherever you happen to be, whatever you happen to be doing. But if you want the mantram to come to your rescue when you need it, if you want it to steady your mind in times of turmoil, you need to practice, practice, practice in calm weather.

Whenever you get a moment free, unless you are doing something that requires attention, repeat your mantram to yourself silently, in the mind – while waiting, walking, washing dishes, and especially when falling asleep at night. Constant repetition drives the mantram deep into consciousness, where it can anchor your mind so surely that no amount of agitation can sweep you away.

I must have given this advice a million times, but it can never be repeated too often. Throughout my life, no matter how assiduously I practiced this skill, I have always been able to find more time, additional opportunities to put it to use. This is how we can gradually extend sovereignty over the mind.

This protective influence can even extend to the body, as I can illustrate with another story from that stormy ocean voyage.

From my first day on board that P&O liner, I acquired a reputation as a very odd bird. For one thing, I had to have my meditation every morning – and since my little cabin was cramped and airless, I chose to huddle in a blanket up on the sports deck, which was quite deserted at dawn. That alone secured the amused attention of some young Australians, whose boredom found relief in making cracks at my expense.

Then, after my meditation, I would take a long, fast walk

STORY

Fear of Flying

Natalie, a software engineer, has been learning to calm her mind to deal with an anxiety that millions of us can relate to.

"At some point in the early nineties, as a result of seeing several scary airplane crash movies, I became very scared of flying. Not so scared that I couldn't get on a plane to go somewhere, but scared enough to have sweaty palms, nausea, and plenty of anxious thoughts.

"This was a situation that definitely needed the mantram, but I wasn't using one in those days and didn't recognize that using it could help me with this massive fear.

"Now I start saying the mantram before I even arrive at the airport, during takeoff, landings, definitely when there's turbulence (or sometimes worse – odd noises!) and even

repeating my mantram to myself – a habit I must have picked up from Mahatma Gandhi's example many years earlier. Of course, a long, fast walk on a relatively small liner means going around and around and around . . . at the pace of an Olympic walker. More opportunities for amusement for my fellow passengers, who much preferred their deck chairs. After a few days of this, my reputation was assured.

Then the storm struck – and when the view started gyrating wildly between sky and sea, my stomach began to behave the same way. I made it through the first day, but the next morning I

while just cruising comfortably. Using my mantram during these times of intense fear has helped to drive it deeper into my consciousness and has made it possible for me to fly with less anxiety. I still get scared, but the mantram lets me bear with the situation.

"I realize now that every time I fly, some part of me is coming face to face with my fear of death. After so many opportunities to repeat my mantram when I fly, my thinking regarding this fear has started to change. It's shifting from 'God, please don't let me die! I'm not ready to die yet' to 'God, may we all arrive safely at our destination today. But if for some reason we don't, help me to keep repeating your name and go straight to you if my time is up.' This is a huge change in my perspective. I'm not free of the fear . . . but I'm seeing how well the mantram works in dealing with it."

– Natalie M., Washington

awoke with the sinking sensation that my time had come. My first impulse was to grab a brown bag and join the others draped miserably over the rails.

But my mantram had awakened too – "Rama, Rama, Rama" – without any conscious prompting. After all those years of practice, it knew when I needed help.

Clinging to the mantram as tightly as to the handrail, I man-

STORY

The Year of the Mantram

Before his heart attack, Chuck had been repeating his mantram "on occasion," such as when falling asleep. It was the pain and stress of hip surgery that drilled the mantram in. Because of that, it was there to help him two months later when the chest pains started – making this "the year the mantram moved to stage center in my life."

"When my wife, Lynn, and I arrived at the emergency room, we rushed inside and within minutes I was diagnosed with a heart attack. They injected me with blood clot thinner and wheeled me to an area dominated by a huge overhead fluoroscope. I kept repeating my mantram and actually followed as the cardiologist worked a catheter toward the area of worst blockage – the main artery. It was 90 to 95 percent blocked. The pain was intense at this point, and I was clinging to the mantram.

"When the cardiologist dissolved the major blockage, I had a sudden, wonderful sense of release. The whole knot of pain in my chest opened like a flower. To that moment, things had seemed terribly dark and bleak.

"After the clot was dissolved, they

aged to reach the sports deck without incident and sat down for meditation. For a while it was touch and go. But then my mind settled down, and I got absorbed in what mystics call the "sea of peace" within.

When I finished and opened my eyes, my stomach had stopped complaining. It had calmed down along with my mind. I felt on top of the world. With the ship still pitching wildly, I sauntered

put me into a hospital bed to await surgery. I slept for one hour only. It was an exceedingly long night – long enough, it seemed to me, for the creation of the world.

"The tension preceding the surgery was monumental: if the operation went wrong, I'd simply be swept away. I have no way of knowing how many mantrams were silently spoken during those hours, but surely there were hundreds, maybe thousands.

"Early the next day, Lynn arrived in time for us to meditate together before one of the nurses started prepping me for surgery. She gave me some potent pills and by the time she wheeled me out, I was almost asleep. Just before the elevator doors closed behind the nurse and me, I heard her tell Lynn that all the operating room staff approaches heart surgery as a spiritual experience. I knew then I was in good hands.

"When I came out of anesthesia, I started the mantram again and it carried me through recovery, just as it still carries me through the tensions and turmoil of my daily life. Now, even recalling this experience reminds me of the vivid sense of joy and opportunity I felt when I came out of the anesthesia and realized I'd survived."

– Chuck C., Oregon

as best I could into the dining room and sat down to a first-rate breakfast – in solitary dignity, monarch of all I surveyed.

The purser looked on in awe. When I rose to go, he approached with new respect and asked in a conspirator's whisper, "What tablets do you use?"

I wanted to tell him, "It's not the stomach that needs to be settled. It's the mind."

> A steady mind has resources for every crisis. You don't need to analyze the causes – just learn to steady your mind.

As far as the mind is concerned, the cause of stress is not particularly important. What matters are the waves of agitation in the mind. Whether we feel anxious, panicky, angry, afraid, or simply out of control, the mind is doing the same thing: heaving up and down like the sea.

This is a precious clue. It means that we don't have to prepare for one kind of crisis in this way and another in that way. All we have to do is learn to steady the mind.

We learn this with little challenges – the thousand and one daily irritations that upset us even when we know they aren't worth getting upset over. Whenever someone cuts in front of you in traffic, repeat the mantram and don't react. Whenever someone contradicts you, repeat your mantram and hold your tongue. Life graciously provides us with innumerable little incidents like this, which instead of irritants can become opportunities for gaining strength. If you go on taking advantage of them as they arise, you can gradually raise your threshold of upsettability higher and higher, until hassles take one look and run away.

Of course, there is much more to life than "small stuff." Coping with hassles is just training. The Olympic challenges are the crises and tragedies – accidents, illness, separation, betrayal, bereavement – that are bound to come to all of us in one form or other without warning. That is when we need to know how to find strength within ourselves, for that is just when external supports are likely to fail.

> The most important lesson to learn from crisis is to find your center of strength within.

If I may offer my own small example, I have been struck by very severe blows in the course of my life. But it is from those trials that I learned to go deep inside myself for strength and consolation. It was a storm of personal tragedies that caused me to turn inward and learn to meditate. This is the real lesson to learn from crisis: not to rely on any external support, but to find your center of strength within.

"Emergencies and crises," the psychologist William James observed, "show us how much greater our vital resources are than we had supposed." This is the opportunity that crisis and challenge offer us. Every one of us has capacities inside us that we have never even dreamed of, which we can learn to draw on in our daily lives. That is our legacy as human beings.

The purpose of this book is to help you get started on the great adventure of claiming this legacy. As a meditation teacher, I have to point out that this is the purpose of meditation, which I have explained in other books. Here I want to focus on skills you can apply right away: simple techniques that anyone can use to banish worry and anxiety, stay calm under pressure, and live each moment to its fullest – and, most significantly, radiate that newfound calm to everyone around.

KEY IDEAS

Chapter One: Strength in the Storm

1. We can't control life, but we can control how we respond to life's challenges. The answer lies in stabilizing the mind.

2. We already have the capacity to deal with challenges. But we need a calm mind to draw on the resources locked up within.

3. The mantram is a key tool for steadying the mind. It's not just mechanical repetition – you learn to trust it by using it.

4. A steady mind has the resources to meet any crisis – no matter what the cause. You don't have to analyze each crisis separately; just use the mantram and you can calm the mind.

5. The most important lesson to learn from crisis is to find your center of strength within.

POINTS TO PRACTICE

Choosing & Using a Mantram

The mantram is the key to all the skills and strategies in this book. If you feel ready to start, here are some suggestions:

1. Choose a mantram established by long tradition. Select one from the list below, or from our Web site at www.easwaran.org/mantrams. A mantram given to the world by Francis of Assisi or the Buddha has great power. Don't make up your own.

Every religious tradition has a mantram, often more than one. You needn't subscribe to any religion to benefit from the mantram, however. You simply have to be willing to try it.

- For Christians, the name of Jesus and the Jesus Prayer – "Lord, Jesus Christ, Son of God, have mercy on us" – are ancient mantrams. Catholics also use *Hail Mary* or *Ave Maria* (not the full "Hail Mary," just those two words).
- Jews may use *Barukh attah Adonai* ("Blessed art thou, O Lord") or *Ribono shel olam* ("O Lord of the universe").
- Muslims repeat the name of Allah or *Bismillah ir-Rahman ir-Rahim* ("In the name of God, Merciful, Compassionate").
- Probably the oldest Buddhist mantram is *Om mani padme hum*, referring to the "jewel in the lotus" of the heart.
- In Hinduism, one of the oldest and most popular mantrams is the one used by Mahatma Gandhi: *Rama, Rama* – a name for God meaning the source of joy within.

What if you don't want a mantram from your own tradition?

Many people are allergic to the religion of their childhood. In such cases, if no other mantram on the list appeals to you, *Rama* is simple, powerful, and carries no negative associations. You can never go wrong with *Rama*.

2. Once you've chosen a mantram, you're ready to give it a good test run. Start by making it part of your day. Repeat your mantram silently to yourself whenever you have an opportunity. Remember, the more you use it, the more it will sink in. Here are some ideal times:

- While walking or jogging
- While waiting in lines or stalled in traffic jams
- Whenever you feel angry, anxious, upset, or afraid
- While doing mechanical chores like washing dishes
- And especially when you are falling asleep

During the day, the mantram will help keep you relaxed and alert. When you fall asleep in it, the mantram will go on working for you throughout the night as well.

One important exception: don't repeat the mantram when you are doing something that requires attention, such as chopping vegetables or driving a car. That's the time to keep focused on what you are doing!

INSPIRATION

Let Nothing Upset You

Let nothing upset you.
Let nothing frighten you.
Everything is changing;
God alone is changeless.
Patience attains the goal.
Who has God lacks nothing;
God alone fills every need.

– SAINT TERESA OF AVILA

CHAPTER TWO

Be at Peace in the Moment

Hurry blocks our access to our deeper resources. One of life's most precious skills is learning to slow down and live completely in the present moment.

The Sanctity of the Present Moment

Introduction by Christine Easwaran

Recently we got an appeal that packed the desperation of the times into just one line: "I need to decompress – my stress level is insane! Help!"

Jean-Pierre de Caussade, a seventeenth-century Catholic priest, offers help in what he calls "the sacrament of the present moment." Every time I read that phrase I'm reminded of how significant each moment is. Most of us are aware of this, but it's so difficult to keep it in mind as time rushes us along. Tragically, we may need a crisis to remind us of what really matters because we're so busy keeping up with all the things that don't.

One of our friends, Jane, is a psychotherapist – one of many professionals who not only practice Easwaran's program themselves but find it useful in their work. Jane recently sketched the kind of life she sees her clients dealing with. It's a composite picture but one we all recognize, in others if not in ourselves:

Many couples come to therapy after realizing that they are disconnected from their partner and coexist or live parallel lives. She has a stressful position at the bank; he is a health care consultant who leaves Monday morning and returns Thursday night. The children are picked up after school at six or carpooled to soccer or dance, picking up burgers at the drive-through on the way. Then there's homework or staying up too late to finish the laundry or work on that report. The next day, after they hit the snooze button several times, the rat race begins again.

Our days don't have to be like this, even in today's frantic world. Slowing down is within the reach of everyone. Not only that, it opens the door to peace of mind, a rich sense of fulfillment, and even joy – while helping us be actually more effective in how our time is used.

Heather, a longtime friend in Canada, learned this in one of the most challenging environments I can think of: as a hospital nurse, where skilled professionals prize the ability to do lots of things at once and do them *fast.*

Sometimes I can't believe the chaos that goes on day after day on a hospital ward. Medications have to be given on time. Patients ring their call bells and you have to respond. Machines and phones and doctors and visitors and family – it's a chaotic environment.

I took great pride in doing as much as I could as fast as I could. But I used to wonder: How can this be healing? Most patients are in pain, afraid, tired. This just adds to their discomfort and anxiety.

Then I heard Easwaran speak at a meditation retreat, and I went back to work determined to slow down.

> *It wasn't easy. When you're immersed in an important task and a call bell rings, you tend to rush in with the attitude "What do you want?" and your mind still on what you had been doing. Now, I started just paying attention to the patients and giving them what they needed.*
>
> *The rest of the staff didn't get what I was doing. They were rushing around, and when they saw me not rushing around so much they wondered if I was really doing the job. Some of them resented that I didn't seem to be carrying my load.*
>
> *But I found I was actually getting more done – and without all that rushing. It surprised even me. Others began to notice too, and their attitude changed. They saw that the call bell rang less frequently and the care I gave was more effective. When a patient is given undivided attention, they don't ring the call bell as often. They seem to be more relaxed, even in a not-so-relaxed atmosphere.*

In years gone by, whenever he saw work pressures mounting around him, Easwaran would frequently walk through the workplace smiling but silent, a quiet reminder to slow down and focus on the task at hand. He was a model of moving without hurry with unshakable concentration, never rushed by circumstance. In whatever he did he was all there, completely absorbed in the present. Instead of being driven by time, he was its master.

In this chapter he explains why slowing down gives us more time instead of depriving us of it – and, as always, offers practical suggestions from his life for how to cultivate this vital skill.

Be at Peace in the Moment

By Eknath Easwaran

One of the curious games I learned as a Boy Scout was musical chairs. There would be thirteen of us and only twelve chairs, and we would all circle around while someone sang our Scout song. Whenever the singer stopped, everyone had to find a seat – and of course, one boy would be without.

Each time around, one more chair would be taken away. As the game got faster and faster, we would begin to push each other and do all kinds of impossible things like trying to jump on a chair from behind, panicky because we were afraid we'd be out of the game.

Many people seem to treat life like this. Time keeps taking away the chairs, and we run around in more and more of a panic trying to get a seat – even if it means someone else will have to go without.

But in every age and culture there are a few – people like Francis of Assisi, Teresa of Avila, Mahatma Gandhi – who find this approach to life as meaningless as the game. After a few rounds of scurrying like the rest of us, they quietly step aside.

Like children, we might feel sorry for them. "Poor Francis! He can't run around any more." But we have to admit they seem to enjoy their choice. Great spiritual figures like these go through life without fuss and frenzy as if they had all the time in the world, and their lives seem so much richer than ours that we have to stop and wonder why. They even seem to accomplish more, so that their lives have enduring value, meaning, and the power to inspire.

Where does this sense of fullness come from? How can such people live without hurry but make each moment count? The Buddha would give a simple answer: it is because they live completely in the present – the only time there is.

STORY

Slowing Down to Catch Up

"I was running late to get to a meditation retreat about 185 miles away. I was riding my motorcycle, and because I was behind I exceeded the speed limit as often as possible by as much as I dared. (Above 85 mph the highway patrol can take you to jail.) My speed resulted in my arrival at the retreat house after 3.5 hours pretty tired and feeling a bit sheepish about leaving things so late that I had to hurry in the first place. On the way home I decided to go no faster than the speed limit and say the mantram whenever I was tempted to speed up. I arrived home quite rested 3.5 hours later.

"This reminded me what a waste of time it is to hurry somewhere. It not only takes me away from whatever's happening right now, but can also put me and others in dangerous circumstances."

– Jack D., California

By contrast, most of us live very little in the present. If we could watch our thoughts, we would be surprised to see how much time we spend in the past or future – or simply daydreaming, out of time altogether. And when we do focus on the present, we try to fit in several things at once. Very seldom can we say we are fully present in the present moment.

Yet, to repeat, now is the only time there is. The present is all we have. If we feel we don't have enough time, the first thing to do is not throw it away. Instead of ceding it to the past and future, we can take steps to give our undivided interest to here and now.

In practice, this means we need to learn to slow down and give complete attention to whatever we are doing. And of course we need to be clear about our priorities, so that what we do is chosen wisely. From this perspective, this book presents a set of skills for living fully here and now.

> Now is the only time there is. If we feel we don't have enough time, the first thing to learn is not to waste the time we have.

Time travel is a staple of science fiction. There is something endlessly fascinating about being able to visit the past or future, perhaps make a few improvements, and come back wiser for what one learned. Imagine having a vehicle that could travel forward or backward in time as easily as a car travels through space. How tempting to be able to go back and fix up history the way it ought to be, undo a past injustice or mistake, or slip into the future to check on investments and then dash back to make a fortune. It seems like such a good way to make the most of time.

The truth is that all of us already have a vehicle like this: our own mind. When we nurse a resentment or dwell on an anxiety, we are stepping into a private time machine and whisking ourselves away from the here and now. Whenever we rehash old experiences, whether pleasant or painful, we have left the present and are traveling in the past. Every fear or anxiety or wishful fantasy is a trip into the future. And just as we can go out to the garage, step into the car, and drive off wherever we like, the mind can escape in its time machine whenever it likes. There is always gas in the tank for trying to get away from here and now.

Most of us spend much more time doing this than we think. And with every trip, we are training the mind not to remain in the present, but to wander in the past and future as aimlessly as in a dream.

Everybody likes to bask in pleasant memories – the time we won all those trophies, prom night, the day we were chosen Manager of the Year. Unfortunately, the past is not always pleasant. And whenever we train the mind to dwell on pleasant memories, we are training it to get caught in unpleasant ones too: the time we finished last, or did something ridiculous we'd like to forget, or hurt or were hurt by someone we loved. This is the stuff of resentment, anxiety, self-deprecation, guilt, and fear, which can make life a terrible burden.

The same is true of the future too. Particularly when we are young – in our teens, twenties, even thirties – there is a tragic tendency to live in anticipation of some future event we think will bring us happiness. A child can hardly wait to become a teenager. Teenagers can hardly wait to get out of high school so they can go to college or get married and honeymoon on Molokai or get a job with an airline and visit faraway lands. When they do land a job, they look forward to a promotion. And on the job, promotion or not, they can't wait for vacation.

> Whenever we daydream, worry, or nurse a grudge, we are training the mind to escape from the present moment. We get trapped in the past or the future.

I know people who wish away all the workdays of the week just to slip away for the weekend to their vacation home in the woods. Those five workdays they are not really alive, because they are not living in the present.

Similarly, many people put in their time absentmindedly for fifty weeks a year while dreaming of the two weeks they can spend in Acapulco. When you let your mind do this, by the time you reach Acapulco you will be thinking, "The Galapagos! Those big tortoises! *That's* what I really want to see." Then you are not alive in Acapulco either, and if you do get to the Galapagos and meet one of those tortoises face to face, you will probably already be thinking about the penguins in Patagonia.

This is what I mean when I say we are trapped in time. At such times we are neither here nor there, neither in Acapulco nor in the Galapagos. The mind has been conditioned to be somewhere, anywhere, else – which means, really, nowhere and never.

Beneath the surface level of consciousness, perhaps one third of our attention is imprisoned in the past – in vain regrets, futile lamentations, nostalgic memories. "If only I could become twenty-five again, with the glow of youth on my cheeks and the sparkle in my eyes, what would I not do?" This sort of thing.

And another third is trapped in the future. "Just wait till I get my degree. After that let me become president. Then let me get the Nobel Prize, and then finally let me become the dictator of the whole world. Then I am going to be happy." It sounds ridiculous, but if we could listen in on our thoughts this is the kind of thing we would hear.

The conclusion is unavoidable: if one third of our time, with all its energy and creative resources, is trapped in the past, and another third is trapped in the future, we are one-third people. That's all of us that is here and now.

I started to understand this when I began to meditate. Meditation is a kind of glass-bottom boat for observing the mind, and when I saw what was happening under the surface, I decided I didn't want to be a one-third person. I wasn't even content to be a two-thirds person. I wanted to be whole, to be full.

In the Indian scriptures there is a glorious verse: "Take fullness from fullness; fullness still remains." That is what I wanted. When you are full, you can give to everyone and still be full. You can love each person and still have love to give to everyone else. You can give fullness away like a millionaire scattering largesse. You can open a flea market for love, setting up a little stand and saying, "Take as much as you can. Help yourself!" and at the end of the day you will still be full.

> The mantram helps us come back to the present moment and focus fully on what we're doing. It makes us more effective.

The mantram can enable us to attain this state of fullness. With practice, we can train the mind to withdraw attention from the past and future whenever it strays there, until we rest completely in the present. Every time the mind wanders – as it surely will – you simply bring it back with the mantram and focus again on what you are doing.

Most wandering thoughts can be traced to past or future. "I don't like the way he behaved to me this morning. I wonder what she meant by that remark last summer. How am I going to face my boss when I haven't got that report done?" This is how the mind runs off, away from the present moment.

For example, you sit down for work and soon a little part of your mind taps you on the shoulder and whispers, "Hey, we're going to a movie tonight! You almost forgot." Instead of letting your mind wander to the coming evening, bring it back to what you are doing. If you let it wander during the morning's work, it will wander in the evening too. When the time comes to see the film, you will be only partially there.

Or perhaps you are trapped in a boring meeting. The clock on the wall says ten-thirty in the morning, but for you it is already eight in the evening and you're saying hello to your date. Your mind is not on the meeting; you scarcely hear the words. While your colleagues talk, you sit there waiting for the sun to set.

And probably your date is doing the same. Imagine: two people who want to be fully alive spending most of the day being anywhere but here and now.

Feeling Stressed Out? Three Tools to Try

How can we make better use of our time without feeling yet more pressure? In this chapter and the next, you'll find three key tools. They each work well on their own, but they're even better used in combination.

The Mantram It's invisible, it's portable, and it offers instant help. Repeat it silently anywhere, at any time. Use it as a "rapid focus tool" to bring the mind back to the present. You'll then have all your resources at your disposal to tackle any challenge you're facing – whether it's an everyday problem, such as a tired child or stalled traffic, or a major crisis.

Slowing Down Hurry makes us tense and causes us to make mistakes. When you are concentrated and slow, you'll do a much better job. It's hard when everyone around you seems so speeded up, but try going against the current: next time you're under pressure, make a deliberate effort to slow down physically and mentally. (The secret is to remember to do it!)

We think this kind of daydreaming is romantic, but it is just the opposite. If you really want to know how to love, you will want to give your beloved your full attention – which means gaining some control over your mind, teaching it to listen to you.

And that means you have to train it. After all, you have been teaching it just the opposite all your life, letting it do whatever it likes. Now you have to teach your mind some new habits. In

One-Pointed Attention This means giving full attention to the task at hand. It sounds straightforward, but the mind loves doing lots of things at once. More on this and how to train your mind to be more focused in chapter 3. In the meantime, try doing only one thing at a time and note the results in your performance.

Perseverance Pays!

Here's the tricky bit. You will see immediate results with all these tools, but the real benefits only emerge over the longer term. You have to be patient with your mind. It's like an untrained puppy; it won't come to heel the first time you call it. You have to persevere. But if you can keep going, you can expect to find:

- More energy (because you're not wasting it on old resentments, fantasies, or worry)
- More concentration (you'll find it easier to plan and prioritize)
- More creativity (once your mind has quieted, it will generate some really good ideas)
- More peace of mind (you'll be calmer, you'll listen better, relationships will improve, and you'll be able to make a richer contribution to life around you)

that meeting, for example, you can start paying attention to what your manager wants to say about efficiency instead of daydreaming about what you're going to do that evening. If the mind starts to wander, you bring it back to the speaker.

You can see how difficult this is. But if you can do it, when you and your beloved finally get together that evening, you will know you can give your complete attention, without the slightest flicker. I can assure you that your date will appreciate it too.

And the next day, instead of replaying the highlights of the evening, you give all your attention to what's on your desk. That too sounds unromantic – and no fun at all. But it is the secret of a free mind, which is the key to romance and happiness as well as to success at your job.

For most of us, the mind doesn't behave like this. Roz and Orlando go out for pizza for a romantic evening, but all Orlando can think about is his project deadline. "We'll lose the contract if we don't ship next week. What's P. H. going to say?" He may not even hear Rosalind complaining, "What's the matter with you tonight? Your mind is somewhere else." If Orlando were honest he would agree: "It's true. I'm not here. I'm in the middle of next week."

And the following day, he may not be able to concentrate on the project any better than on Rosalind. His mind will keep slipping away to what went wrong the night before. As the Buddha might say, "When you are with a date, be with your date. When you are at work, work. Don't wobble."

We can train the mind to rest in the present – by listening really attentively to others, for instance.

How can you achieve this kind of concentration? Once you understand the ways of the mind, every day provides opportunities for learning to rest in the present moment. I can illustrate with some examples from my own experience.

First, when somebody is being critical of you, your mind will naturally tend to skitter away. That is the natural response of the mind to any painful experience. One of the most powerful ways to teach your mind to remain in the present is to give all your attention to what that person is saying, even if it is something you do not like to hear. And don't take your eyes off that person, either. A wandering eye is a sure sign of a wandering mind.

I learned this skill at faculty meetings, which provide an endless variety of opportunities for being contradicted. Opinions that could have no conceivable importance outside a campus are often attacked and defended so fiercely that you'd think the fate of the world hung on the outcome.

In discussions like these, before I learned to use a mantram, if someone were critical of my views on Shakespeare's use of poetry in drama, I used to get upset and avoid that person – a natural, normal human response.

But once I understood that the real issue was training the mind, I learned to do just the opposite. Instead of avoiding my critic, I would go out of my way to sit next to him in the faculty room and say, "Please tell me more about your views on verse drama. And you don't need to pull punches – I'd really like to know." I would listen carefully to every word, doing my best to attend with concentration and not interrupt with my own views.

This proved to be a marvelous exercise. Sometimes, of course, I learned from it – but even when I did not, it helped immensely in training the mind, which was my real goal. The gain in security was immeasurable. Whatever the challenge, I found, you can learn to listen with concentration and respect for opposing views – and of course, at the same time, you can learn to state your own views with concentration and respect as well.

STORY

Quiet Patience the Victor in Boardroom Battle

"Last month I presented what was almost my last treasurer's report for a local nonprofit. The board of this organization is a confident, successful, wealthy group, and I was certainly in the lower tier of all these characteristics! One of the trustees is extremely critical and always has something nasty to say about the reports. This time she picked apart every line. I felt humiliated, like a low-level, incompetent employee, in front of all these successful business people. I was about to throw my papers across the table, say some very harsh words, and storm out in a rage when I remembered Easwaran. I closed my mouth, said my mantram, and accepted her request for changes.

"After the meeting, instead of simply leaving with my hurt feel-

Second, I would suggest, try to work cheerfully with concentration at jobs you dislike. I call this "playing with likes and dislikes." Most of our personal preferences, you know, are not particularly significant. Training the mind to go against what it likes and dislikes – for example, doing something you dislike that benefits others – is a most effective way of teaching your mind to rest in the present and enjoy it.

For me, campus proved to be an excellent place to practice this. People think literature teachers are always reading novels, but a lot of the job is plain drudgery. On my campus, we had plenty of paperwork but only one secretary for the whole department, and

ings, I found myself walking up to her with a smile and kind words. (The words must have come from somewhere else; I have never had that kind of grace under pressure.) She said, 'Oh, my dear, your heart must sink when you see me walk into meetings!'

"Her health was very poor, so without conscious volition I said, 'Oh, no, I am just glad you are able to come. And whenever you comment on the reports, they are always better as a result.' I don't know if she felt better, but I certainly did. It was hard to concentrate on the person rather than her remarks, but I felt very strengthened by not acting defensive.

"After that, people came up to me wondering how I had managed to be so calm under such provocation. I had only been humiliated in my own mind – no one else had seen things that way at all!"

– Karen H., Colorado

on top of that each of us had a full load of teaching chores such as reading a hundred and fifty freshman essays on *Romeo and Juliet* and marking the same misspellings over and over.

Most of us on the faculty had a tendency to postpone paperwork, and as for reading student papers, my mind would usually

STORY

Learning from Toddlers

Michelle's three small children give her lots of daily opportunities to resist multitasking.

"I often get caught up in the cycle of all the things I have to do, and in this speeded-up, task-driven mind-set, I get impatient and frustrated by constant bids for attention that keep me from 'getting my work done.'

"Young children are one-pointed and slowed down by nature. When I can see things from their perspective, it's a surprising relief from the tyranny of my own speeded-up thinking. When I can let go of what I'm doing and answer the insistent tug on my jeans to 'look, look, look at the woly-poly bug, Mama,' I can slow down enough to have a little flash of real contentment and happiness. In that moment I can experience the elusive bliss of just being, that 'all will be well' sensation. My toddler teaches me that!

"What is so amazing is how quickly I forget that being speeded up and many-pointed is painful and I get right back on my treadmill, trying to create happiness and well-being in my life by checking off my list. I guess that's why they call it spiritual practice, *right?"*

– Michelle O., California

come up with the same old thought: "I don't like this! If we can't put it off, let's get it over with as quickly as possible so we can do something interesting." You should have seen the look on my mind's face when I began to reply, "I don't care if you don't like it. We're going to give complete attention to this task even if it seems like drudgery."

> Attention doesn't wander because a job is dull. It's the other way around: a job seems dull when we allow our attention to wander.

Then I made an even more surprising discovery: by giving them my full attention, such jobs actually lost their drudgery. Many even became interesting. I had got it backwards: attention doesn't wander because something is dull; life seems dull when attention wanders. Again, full attention was the key.

Time has been illustrated as an infinite cosmic carpet that is always rolled up behind and before us. One day comes and it is unrolled from the future, and that evening it is rolled up again. The only part of the carpet that is open is the present moment.

The Buddha would go farther. There is no such thing as the past, he would say. It has been rolled up; it doesn't exist. Nothing remains of it but what we hold in our minds. And there is no such thing as the future; it has not yet been rolled out.

That is why attention flowing to the past is energy wasted. We are dumping our vitality into a black hole! The same is true of the future: looking forward to pleasant events, worrying about unpleasant ones, fantasizing about dreams coming true is simply energy drained away, like letting your car idle in the garage all night. When the mind stays in the present, all this vitality comes back to us.

> Time does not hurry us; we hurry ourselves.
> If we could slow the mind down, we would see
> that there is never any moment but the present,
> never any time but now.

The very pressure of time is an illusion, the Buddha would say, created by the rushing movement of the mind. Time does not hurry us; we hurry ourselves. If we could slow the mind down, we would see that there is never any moment but the present, never any time but now.

The application is utterly practical. When you bring the rushing process of the mind to a healing stillness, you rest completely in each moment. You give your very best each moment, without any loss of vitality to past or future.

There is no anxiety in this state, for you have nothing to lose. There is no craving for personal satisfaction; you are completely full. And in each moment you are free. If someone says something unkind, it has no connection with what you think or say in return. You don't react to people; you are free to choose your response – free to be loving always. This is the ultimate significance of resting fully in the present moment.

KEY IDEAS

Chapter Two: Be at Peace in the Moment

1. Now is the only time there is. If we feel we don't have enough time, the first thing to learn is not to waste the time we have.

2. Whenever we daydream, worry, or nurse a grudge, we are training the mind to escape from the present moment. We get trapped in the past or future.

3. The mantram helps us come back to the present moment and focus fully on what we're doing. It makes us more effective.

4. We can train the mind to rest in the present – by listening really attentively to others, for instance.

5. Attention doesn't wander because a job is dull. It's the other way around – a job seems dull when we allow our attention to wander.

6. Time does not hurry us; we hurry ourselves. If we could slow the mind down, we would see that there is never any moment but the present, never any time but now.

POINTS TO PRACTICE

Slowing Down

When life gets too full, we spend the day racing past the people we love in order to get our To Do list done. Haven't you known people who've spent a whole life like this, and end up with lots done but no one truly loved? We can avoid this by slowing down and setting priorities. The quality of life goes from black-and-white to Technicolor.

1. "Most of us think too much about what we should do," said Meister Eckhart, "and not enough about what we should be. If we would pay more attention to what we should be, our work would shine forth brightly."

How about making another list, but not just for today or even for this week? Make it a To Be list for this life. Ask yourself: By the end of my life, what kind of person do I want to have become? What personal qualities would I like people to remember me for?

This is *your* list – no one else has to see it. Be honest and put down only things you really care about. Revise it as you use it, to make it work for *you*. Your own language is probably more helpful than a laundry list of perfections. For example, it might be more useful to start with specifics like "Be more sympathetic, esp. to Nate and Megan" than with something general like "Be kind."

The way to get a To Be list completed *on time* (by the end

of this life!) is to be sure it's next to your To Do list every day. With this as your guide, try out the following exercises:

2. Take time right now to think about your daily schedule. Find part of your day when you could slow down if you wanted to. It might be:

- During your lunch break with your colleagues
- When the kids get home from school
- Each time you greet a client or patient

Try it out this week. When your "slowing down time" arrives, say your mantram a couple of times and consciously slow down. Give your attention to those around you. At the end of the week, reflect on the experience. Was it helpful?

3. Write your To Do list for today. (Be sure it takes into account your To Be list also.) Are any items really unnecessary? If so, cross them out.

Which of the remaining items would you prefer to avoid? Put that one at the top of the list. Do it with gusto. (To make a dull job interesting, focus on it.) What's your experience?

4. Experiment with "Slowing Down to Catch Up" (page 40). When you start rushing to get somewhere, thinking about being late instead of what you're doing, repeat the mantram to slow down and focus. See if you actually get there as fast as you would have by speeding up – and with less stress.

INSPIRATION

I Weave a Silence

I weave a silence onto my lips.
I weave a silence into my mind.
I weave a silence within my heart.
I close my ears to distractions.
I close my eyes to attractions.
I close my heart to temptations.
Calm me, O Lord, as you stilled the storm.
Still me, O Lord; keep me from harm.
Let all tumult within me cease.
Enfold me, Lord, in your peace.

– A GAELIC PRAYER

CHAPTER THREE

Take the Worry Away

Living completely in the present is also the most joyful way to be free from worry and anxiety. And one of the simplest ways to do this is to do only one thing at a time.

Full Attention

Introduction by Christine Easwaran

I hear so many people today say their lives feel out of control. I find this one of the most disturbing symptoms of our times, and it can be traced directly to anxiety over trying to do too much. We try to squeeze more into our days than can possibly be done, and that means more to worry about: all the things we have to do, all the things we wish we *could* do, how little time we have to do it in and what will happen if we don't manage – and whether we are up to it anyway . . .

"For months now," one woman said at one of our retreats,

> *I've been feeling anxious about every blessed thing – my children, my relationships, money problems, closets out of control, my weight, my skin, whatever. I just can't turn off my mind. At the end of the day I'm exhausted and my brain still won't shut up, so now I can't sleep – so I worry about that too. My work is beginning to suffer because I'm having trouble keeping my mind on the job, and that's maybe the biggest worry of all. It's scary – I feel like I'm going into a tailspin.*

This is so familiar that it might be a litany for our modern world.

What a refreshing contrast to read words like these from one of the greatest spiritual teachers of our age:

> *If I did not live from one moment to the next, it would be impossible for me to keep my patience. I can see only the present; I forget the past and I take good care not to worry about the future. We get discouraged and feel despair because we brood about the past and the future. It is such folly to pass one's time fretting, instead of resting quietly on the heart of Jesus.*

If you like, substitute "resting quietly on the present moment" in that last sentence; you will have the meaning just as faithfully. The writer is Thérèse of Lisieux, and if you think that as a nun she was protected from stress, I urge you to read her autobiography. She didn't have to drive her children to soccer games and ballet classes while maintaining a stellar sales performance, but her day was full of difficulties – poor health, tasks beyond her strength, hostility and gossip – that every one of us can recognize and relate to.

Without Thérèse's hard-won gift for living in the present, we are at the mercy of today's fast-paced, desire-driven lifestyle. In such a world, free-floating anxiety and panic attacks are common. Even though we no longer live in a jungle, we still respond anxiously to perceived threats with the old conditioned response of "fight or flight."

In such situations, the mantram is enormously effective as first aid because it reverses this conditioning. As the mantram slows down the mind, the heart rate and breathing rhythm follow. To go beyond first aid, however, we need to free ourselves from the burden of a runaway mind.

Easwaran calls this a "mechanical problem" because it has to do with the machinery of thinking. In this chapter, he addresses this condition with a surprising but powerful solution. If we want to be free from worry, he says, we need to be one hundred percent in the present. And to do that, we need to train the mind to do one thing at a time with complete attention.

Worry, anxiety, fear, regret, guilt, and resentment, Easwaran points out, have a common dynamic: the mind cannot stay focused, but jumps like a grasshopper to all kinds of conflicting, unrelated thoughts. Concentrating on one task at a time focuses attention, which not only results in a better job but actually improves the ability to manage the conflicting claims on attention that are the order of the day – in the emergency room, the classroom, or even the playroom at home.

Recently, confirmation of this idea has been coming from scientific circles. Switching rapidly among unrelated tasks, researchers are finding, is a very inefficient way to use your brain.

Easwaran often joked that if we could learn how to harness worry, there would be no energy crisis. When attention stays in the present, worry actually evaporates, releasing a flood of vitality that we can use to face a problem and deal with it instead of fretting.

"The moments of our daily life may appear commonplace,"

said one of Mahatma Gandhi's closest colleagues, Vinoba Bhave, "but they carry enormous significance." He added that when we look upon every moment as sacred, a new energy flows into our lives. We heard this echoed recently by a young friend in Holland, Anna:

> *The last few months I have been dealing with some ghosts from the past that came to haunt my mind. The interesting thing is that these ghosts tend to turn up in packs, the cowards!*
>
> *My mind can be very persistent in holding on to old pains and memories, so this time I tried to fight them off with a mantram offensive to keep my mind focused and get it off dwelling on myself.*
>
> *With the risk of sounding like a bad commercial, I have to say that the result has been really surprising. In just a few weeks my mind is so much clearer. My compulsive thoughts have less of a grip on me.*
>
> *But that was not the entire lesson. The amazing eye-opener for me is that the fight has released a strange sort of energy. This might sound weird, but it feels like there is more room for love and devotion, and also for thankfulness – all in the form of energy.*
>
> *So now the fight continues, but with more faith and enthusiasm.*

When we look upon each moment as the result of every other moment of our lives, we can seize it as an opportunity to change our thinking and therefore our action. It is a thrilling thought.

Take the Worry Away

By Eknath Easwaran

Sleepwalking is a fascinating phenomenon. I once read about a whole family afflicted with this problem. On one occasion everyone got out of bed, still sound asleep, to go to the kitchen for a midnight snack. In the morning no one could explain where the food in the refrigerator had gone.

The Buddha would call all of us sleepwalkers. We go through the motions of living with little more awareness than someone who is dreaming. If we could watch our thoughts, we would find that instead of being here and now, our attention is constantly wandering everywhere and everywhen else – to the past, to the future, to fantasy lands where reality has never visited. Living in the present is simply a matter of being fully awake, which is what the word *buddha* literally means.

When most of our attention is trapped in the past and future, we are bankrupt for the present. We are complete paupers here and now. That is why, when a little problem comes, we sometimes feel as if we have been crushed by the Himalayas. It is not the problem that burdens us; that is only an anthill. It is the bankruptcy of resources for the present that makes us feel unable to cope with the challenge.

We live where our attention is. When we direct our attention fully to the present moment, we are fully alive.

All of us want to be completely alive, to live one hundred percent in the present moment. What prevents us? More urgently, how can we bring about such a state of mind?

The great American psychologist William James gives us a clue in a quotation I found in a most unexpected place, *Vogue* magazine. (Actually, it was Christine who found it.) This is a direct quotation: "The faculty of voluntarily bringing back a wandering attention, over and over again, is the very root of judgment, character, and will. An education which should include this faculty would be the education *par excellence*."

In that one sentence we have the secret of life: the key to genius, to success, to love, to happiness, to security, to fulfillment. We live where our attention is. If attention wanders all over the map, our lives cannot help being scattered, shallow, and confused. By contrast, complete concentration is the secret of genius in any field. Those who can put their attention on a task or goal and keep it there are bound to make their mark on life.

Attention is also the secret of joy. To enjoy anything, we have to be present. If our attention is scattered or distracted, as when we're hurrying to do several things at once, no one is really there to enjoy the moment. The pleasure an artist finds in nuances of color that the rest of us do not see, a musician's acute enjoyment of harmonies, comes really not from the perceptions but from the capacity to be absorbed in them. When attention is complete, that capacity comes into every moment. Life's ordinary joys are multiplied a thousand times.

STORY

One Small Task, One Big Victory

As a reading tutor, Mike's job is to help students keep bringing attention back when it wanders.

"Distraction comes in many forms. Often, when a task becomes challenging for a student, he or she will focus on a perceived inability to rise to the occasion.

"One of my favorite students – I'll call him Jeremy – fell into this trap during a long study session for a midterm exam. Halfway through the session he refused to do any more. He was on a medication for hyperactivity, and he insisted that the medication had worn off and there was no point in continuing.

"I suggested that we try our best to look at just a small part of the subject matter. After all, I pointed out, we had over an hour to kill. We might as well try to study. If it was a complete failure, I assured him, we could go back to arguing.

"He agreed. We had five chapters to review and we started with the first paragraph of the first chapter. At first he was distracted, but I was able to bring him back to the paragraph, and soon we were both engrossed in the material.

"By the end of the hour, we had finished more than half the reading. No one was more amazed than Jeremy. 'If your medicine wore off, who did that reading?' I asked. Jeremy's only answer was a huge grin."

– Mike S., New Mexico

By one name or another, you will find training attention – "voluntarily bringing back a wandering attention, over and over again" – at the center of every genuine spiritual tradition. The Buddha, for example, placed great emphasis on what he called mindfulness. In other traditions, attention is considered the essence of true prayer. Even if you do nothing in prayer but bring your mind back whenever it wanders, one Catholic mystic says, your time is very well spent.

This is true in every aspect of life, because attention gives value to everything we do. That is why, whenever you recall a wandering attention, you are engaged in what William James called the highest kind of education. I call it training the mind, and it is very much like training a pup. If you try to teach a puppy to obey you for half an hour and then let it do whatever it likes the rest of the day, you will never have a well-behaved pet. Similarly, if you let your mind do whatever it likes, it will chew up your relationships, bully you into indulging it, and generally make a mess of your life.

Here, what I recommend is simple but challenging: do only one thing at a time and give it your full attention. This is the key to doing a good job of any kind, and the secret of learning to live completely in the present moment.

At first, doing just one thing at a time may seem impractical, even nonsensical. But I assure you that it can be done – and that as your mind grows accustomed to giving your best attention to one thing at a time, you will find yourself actually accomplishing more without pressure, burnout, tension, or fatigue.

> Do only one thing at a time and give it complete concentration. This is the key to excellence – and to learning to live in the present.

Training attention begins on the level of physical activity, which corresponds to the most superficial level of the mind. But even there we find we don't have much control because of compulsive distractions, which are the order of the day. The mind likes to be distracted. It is accustomed to wandering. The essential problem in doing one thing at a time is that we don't really want to – or, more accurately, the mind doesn't want to. It is used to doing whatever it likes.

A wandering mind gets bored easily, so it likes to combine a task like brushing teeth with reading the *Wall Street Journal* or listening to a lesson on learning Italian. "Why waste time on your teeth?" the mind wants to know. "Why not do something interesting at the same time?"

Actually, it is doing two things at once that truly wastes time. All we are doing in such cases is teaching the mind to do whatever it chooses.

The problem with this is not found in moments of dental hygiene. It is discovered in times of crisis, when we can't stop thinking about something painful or oppressive no matter how much we desire to. Just when we most need some control over our attention, we are helpless.

Years ago, in San Francisco, Christine and I saw Rodin's statue

The Thinker. A tourist next to us asked the inevitable question: "I wonder what he's thinking about."

STORY

Mantram Dreaming

"For a couple of years after the war, I wasn't able to sleep except in fits and starts. The same nightmares would come and I'd wake up in a cold terror, sweating and shaking all over. I was afraid to go to sleep.

"Finally someone told me about the mantram. I was skeptical, but hey – no side effects, and I was desperate. I especially glommed onto the idea that if I could fall asleep in the mantram, it would go on healing even in my sleep. But when I tried, I couldn't manage to hold on to it and the nightmares would still come.

"I got angry. I thought, 'You're a Marine! You can stay cool under fire; why can't you do this?' So I decided I wasn't going to sleep unless it was with the mantram. That night I didn't go to bed; I just sat up in a chair repeating the mantram. I decided that was my job: not to sleep but to say the mantram.

"Finally I must have dozed off, because I remember feeling that old fear that the nightmare was about to start up again. But that same moment, the mantram started echoing in my mind. It just blew everything else away. I woke up with my heart pounding, but this time it wasn't with fear. I guess I could call it gratitude. I was stark wide awake and at peace. I felt for the first time that I'd be okay.

"The old memories still come, but they're getting weaker. I'm not afraid of the past any more. I think I've fallen asleep in the mantram every night since then, because it's there in the morning when I wake up."

– Robert K., Texas

I wanted to say, "I know. He's thinking, 'How can I stop thinking?'"

Most of us have asked that question when the turmoil of the mind won't let us rest. At such times, we'd give anything to shut down the frantic thought-factory in our heads for just one healing hour. It took years for me to learn the simple answer: to train attention at every opportunity, even in little things, so the capacity is there when we need it.

> Every moment is precious, so don't let the mind wander with routine tasks. Use the mantram instead.

After a while of practicing this, you will make a wonderful discovery: in reality, there *are* no little things. Every moment is unique; every moment is precious. And life is a tapestry of such moments. When we are completely awake in the present, every moment is fresh; nothing is ever stale.

There are, I agree, many times in the day when we are doing mechanical chores – washing dishes, for example – that simply do not require much attention. At such times, use the mantram to keep your awareness in the present while your hands are engaged.

I'm often asked, "Repeat the mantram while washing dishes? Isn't that doing two things at once?" The mind loves intellectual questions like this. What you will discover is that when you are doing something that doesn't require attention, your mind wanders off on its own to as many places as it can. It strays to the past, wonders about the future, worries a little, plans for a second or two and then tunes in to a half-remembered song – whatever happens to come to mind. All this is worse than a waste of time and energy; it scatters your awareness and leaves you anywhere but here and now. The mantram brings you back to the present. Later, when you turn to something you *do* want to give attention to, you will be much more present – which means you will enjoy it more and do a better job.

It's very important, however, not to repeat the mantram when busy with a task that *does* require attention, such as studying, operating tools, or driving. That is the time to put all your attention on the job. Anything less not only divides attention but often invites an accident. Thousands of lives are lost on the road each year, and even experts now connect many traffic accidents with distracted drivers doing something else while behind the wheel, even for a split second.

> Tasks such as driving need full concentration. Put all your attention on the job, even if your body is doing several things at once.

Again, I am often asked if it isn't impossible to do only one thing at a time while driving. Don't such tasks require us to do several things at once, such as scanning the whole field of vision while accelerating, braking, or steering?

The answer is that driving with concentration *is* doing one thing at a time, as any good race car driver will tell you. The same holds true with many familiar activities, such as football or playing the piano. The body may be doing many things, but attention should be completely focused.

I once found a wonderful illustration of this in another unexpected quarter: the *San Francisco Chronicle* sports section on the day after the spectacular climax of Super Bowl XXIII. In the final moments of that game – "two minutes and 39 seconds of pure magic" for football fans – the San Francisco 49ers were behind when Joe Montana, one of the most gifted athletes I have seen, threw a pass for a touchdown run that turned defeat to victory. The crowd went wild, but Montana, as always, stayed cool despite all the pressure. He seemed to have all the time in the world.

Lowell Cohn, writing for the *Chronicle,* hit the mark when he commented, "So what is it that makes Joe special? Just this: Montana has the ability not to get caught up in the emotion of the moment. When other guys feel the sweat on their palms, Montana is totally focused on the next play. No distractions. No sickening fear." Instead of worrying about losing or fantasizing about winning, he just does his best, one hundred percent absorbed in what he is doing.

Then comes the key point, a sure sign of the concentration that marks genius:

"There is something else. Sometimes things happen in slow motion for Joe. At the most crucial times, the world slows down and things get big, and he feels as if he has total control. He was in that world when he threw the winning pass to John Taylor.

"'It happened sort of in slow motion,' Montana admitted. He

had dropped back to pass, and suddenly, everything slowed down and became totally clear. . . . He threw his pass as if only he and Taylor inhabited the field. Then he lost sight of the ball, heard the screams of triumph, and the world returned to normal speed."

After reading that I thought to myself, "If Joe takes to meditation, he'll go far."

One of the most precious benefits this skill brings is the capac-

STORY

Caring from a Calm Perspective

As a pediatrician and mother of three, Stephanie has years of experience with distracting claims on her attention.

"It's a constant struggle, but one of the most valuable things I've learned is that full attention to the problem at hand is the essence of doing a good job, no matter what that job is.

"Now, whenever I have a really sick child in front of me, or a really frightened parent, or a difficult procedure to do, or bad news to convey, the mantram seems to switch on and a feeling of deep calm comes over me which helps me become very focused on taking things one step at a time.

"Sometimes it feels like the situation goes into slow motion so I can take my time and consider things very carefully. Frequently I sense, almost physically, the child and the parents calming down. I feel during these times that I am truly an instrument and a stronger power is taking over the situation. If I felt I was in charge, I would be shaking in my shoes and I wouldn't be able to do my job."

– Stephanie J., Hawaii

ity to live completely in the present, with all your inner resources at your beck and call.

When we dwell on the past, attention is drawn away from the present, which is real, into a time that is not real. The more compelling the memory, the more likely it is that attention will get caught there – which means we have less attention available for real life around us. That is why doing one thing at a time is such a powerful way to live completely in the present.

> Teaching the mind to do one thing at a time with complete attention can lift the burdens of the past and future: regret, resentment, guilt, worry, and anxiety.

This one apparently simple skill can lift the burden of the past. Past injuries, whether real or imagined, gain their power over us from the attention we give them. Without attention, they have no more power than a ghost. It's not at all easy to withdraw attention from a compulsive memory, but every time you try, you weaken the compulsive pull a little, making it easier to break free the next time that memory comes.

This is also the secret of forgiveness. Only when we cease to feed a past injury or injustice with our attention can we truly "forgive and forget." Interestingly enough – and all-important – this includes forgiving ourselves.

In practice, this means that whenever you catch your attention wandering into the past – not only to painful memories but any foray into the past, even replaying pleasant memories – repeat the mantram and bring your attention back to what you are doing here and now. If the pull of the past is compulsive, combine the mantram with a fast walk and then throw yourself into vigorous, concentrated work – preferably something that benefits others, because that will take your mind off yourself. When you do this over and over again, the mantram gradually drains oppressive memories of their emotional charge. You still remember past events, of course, but the memory has no hold on you – because you are no longer holding on to it.

Similarly, fears, anxieties, and insecurities refer to the future. What about our stocks and shares? What about our job? What about this? What about that? No one has ever benefited from worrying like this. The mind is being pulled into the future – which, like the past, is an unreal world, a time that has not yet happened. If we can keep attention focused on what we are doing, thoughts will not stray into the future. Then we simply cannot be plagued by anxieties or uncertainties because they get no attention at all. We will have the confidence to face whatever comes.

KEY IDEAS

Chapter Three: Take the Worry Away

1. We live where our attention is. When we direct our attention fully to the present moment, we are fully alive.

2. Do only one thing at a time and give it complete concentration. This is the key to excellence.

3. Every moment is precious, so don't let the mind wander with routine tasks. Use the mantram instead.

4. Tasks such as driving need full concentration. Put all your attention on the job, even if your body is doing several things at once.

5. Teaching the mind to do one thing at a time with complete attention can lift the burdens of past and future: regret, resentment, guilt, worry, and anxiety.

POINTS TO PRACTICE

One-Pointed Attention

1. Think of the occasions when you habitually do more than one thing at a time. Some of these might be:

- Listening to the radio or using a cell phone while you drive
- Checking e-mail while talking on the phone
- Watching TV while talking with your spouse or friends
- Reading the paper while your seven-year-old tells you about her soccer game

Choose an activity like this that might be better if done with one-pointed attention. Try it that way for a few days. Do you notice any improvements?

2. There's a real difference between unfocused worrying and realistic planning. Planning can be a useful and necessary activity when done with one-pointed attention. Worry isn't useful at all – it's when the mind goes round and round in circles, making you more and more anxious and depressed.

To begin getting rid of unproductive worry, start a mantram worry book. Get yourself a nice blank book, and whenever you find yourself unable to focus on your work because you are worrying about some person or event, write down at the top of a page – in one sentence or less – what your worry is. Then fill the rest of the page with the mantram. Channel your energy away from the worry by giving your complete attention to the mantram. When you're finished, go back to the work at hand with full attention. Don't let worry grab your attention again! Leave your worries in the book.

Give this experiment some time before you evaluate the result. Once your worry book is full, ask yourself, "Was this exercise more beneficial than the same amount of worrying?"

You might even page through the book and glance at the worries you turned over to the mantram. Have your attitudes toward any of these situations changed since you started this exercise? Some worries just fade. Some you gradually come to terms with. With others, you may find you get a clearer view of the underlying problem and can start focused planning.

3. *Mantram Walk:* Here's another activity that helps when you're feeling anxious. Take a really long, really brisk mantram walk – repeating your mantram silently as you go. Walk as fast as is comfortable for you, swinging your arms and taking nice, long strides. Keep the mantram going in rhythm with your step. When your mind tries to dwell on anxious thoughts, bring it back to the mantram and pick up the pace a bit.

Try this prescription for anxiety for two weeks. If the dosage doesn't seem strong enough, double it: make the mantram walks twice as long – and a little more brisk! (The extra effort helps unify your attention.)

INSPIRATION

The Mirror of This World

Every particle of the world is a mirror,
In each atom lies the blazing light
of a thousand suns.
Cleave the heart of a rain-drop,
a hundred pure oceans will flow forth.
Look closely at a grain of sand,
The seed of a thousand beings can be seen.
The foot of an ant is larger than an elephant;
In essence, a drop of water
is no different than the Nile.
In the heart of a barley-corn
lies the fruit of a hundred harvests;
Within the pulp of a millet seed
an entire universe can be found.
In the wing of a fly, an ocean of wonder;
In the pupil of the eye, an endless heaven.
Though the inner chamber of the heart is small,
the Lord of both worlds
gladly makes his home there.

– MAHMUD SHABESTARI

CHAPTER FOUR

Nourish Your Mind

Building a strong body requires good food. The mind, too, needs nourishment to grow stronger. Just as the body is what we eat, the mind absorbs what it experiences. For a healthy body, we avoid junk food. Why not avoid junk experience too?

Healing Peace

Introduction by Christine Easwaran

What strengthens the mind? An early morning walk repeating the mantram, uplifting reading, prayer or meditation – any of these will refresh your spirit, and if you set aside a little time for inner nourishment every day, it will begin to transform your life.

Crowding too much into our days leaves us no time for this kind of refreshment. The chatterbox mind is given no opportunity to learn to be still. In order to find joy in life, the mind must be calm. Even though you may be lounging on a beach in a tropical paradise, if your mind is in turmoil, where is the enjoyment?

Without a deep sense of inner quiet, in fact, most of life loses its taste and value. This kind of profound peace cannot come from anything outside us. It nourishes, heals, and restores us from within. "He leads me beside the still waters," says the Psalmist. "He restores my soul." Our minds need deep nourishment; we know that as intuitively as we know that our bodies need food. But, in the press of things, we forget.

Easwaran often compared our search for fulfillment to a game that children enjoyed when he was growing up. Imagine hide-and-seek played in the rambling old home of a large extended family, more than a hundred strong. The child who is hiding calls out, "Koooeeeeeee!" As the sound echoes through rooms, corridors, and alcoves, the children run here and there searching for its source.

Modern life seems like that game, but much more frantic. Trying to fill our time with activities and pleasures, we race through empty rooms chasing an echo – lost in the echo chamber of the mass media, or the "media mirage," as Easwaran calls it. It never occurs to us to stop, quiet down, and try to perceive clearly the real source of what we seek.

We need to take time every day to return to the source of our fulfillment. We need to slow down and look within for nourishment. For most of us the best time is in the morning, before the rush of the day begins, when the mind tends naturally to be still.

Easwaran and I always got up early, when the day is fresh. To make sure that we were fresh too, we went to bed early. I never felt I missed a thing that way, our mornings were so rich. For many years we enjoyed a daily walk on a nearby beach, where the mantram, silently repeated in our minds, mingled with the sound of the waves. Easwaran used to joke that there were more mantrams on that beach than grains of sand.

When I have a few minutes in the middle of the day, I enjoy filling a page or two with my mantram. It focuses scattered thoughts and quiets my mind. I carry a small notebook for writing the mantram whenever the opportunity arises.

Another form of inner nourishment is uplifting company: the fellowship of people who share your highest ideals and, like you, are trying to live in harmony with them. This needn't mean conformity, and it has nothing to do with political opinions. I have friends who cancel out each other's votes in every election but love and support each other in their highest aspirations. The principle, as Easwaran says here, is simple: try to spend time with people who embody qualities you are trying to strengthen in yourself, because "we become like those we associate with."

Psychologists and physicians know the importance of peer support in trying to change deep-seated habits. The same is true in making interior changes – seeking the peace within that leads to joy. The company of others trying to make similar changes supports and reinforces our own efforts.

That is one reason why people wanting to uplift their lives often go on retreat or spend time in a cloistered setting where the whole atmosphere aims at nourishing mind and spirit. You can create mini-retreats of your own, too, either alone or with a friend. Shut the door to the outside world for a day or a weekend, turn off the phone and TV, and follow a quiet schedule together: mantram walks, reading, whatever nourishes your mind and lets you remember your real priorities.

I can particularly recommend what Christian mystics call *lectio divina,* the slow, deep reading of a favorite scripture, saint, or mystic. You're not reading to acquire information but to absorb wisdom. Easwaran sometimes spent hours like this each day, so that figures like Thérèse of Lisieux and Sri Ramakrishna became living companions for him – the loftiest kind of elevating company.

I like to write out uplifting spiritual passages from the scriptures and mystics of all traditions. The words go in deep when written like this, slowly and with appreciation of their meaning. They become part of your day, and gradually part of your life.

Meditating on such passages is an extremely effective way to nourish the mind at a very deep level. Easwaran's method of meditation involves going slowly through the words of some of the most uplifting spiritual poetry ever composed. He and I always began the day with meditation and ended the day with meditation as well. My friends and I carry on this practice, beginning and ending each day with inspired words such as these, from Saint Augustine:

> *Imagine if all the tumult of the body were to quiet down, along with all our busy thoughts about earth, sea, and air;*
>
> *if the very world should stop, and the mind cease thinking about itself, go beyond itself, and be quite still;*
>
> *if all the fantasies that appear in dreams and imagination should cease, and there be no speech, no sign:*
>
> *And imagine if that moment were to go on and on, leaving behind all other sights and sounds but this one vision which ravishes and absorbs and fixes the beholder in joy:*
>
> *Would this not be what is bidden in scripture,*
> *Enter into the joy of thy Lord?*

Nourish Your Mind

By Eknath Easwaran

Christine and I are fond of old movies, so I once took her to a real classic: *The Garden of Allah,* produced by David O. Selznick just three years before he made movie history with *Gone with the Wind.* It was pure Hollywood, overflowing with talent and flush with Technicolor.

In the story, Marlene Dietrich plays a beautiful woman traveling in the Sahara who meets and falls in love with a man who calls himself "Boris," played by Charles Boyer. But Boris hides a secret: he is really Brother Antonio, who has fled his monastery to seek the pleasures he fancies he lost by seeking God.

As we watch the couple strolling in evening clothes across alluring sands, dining with cut glass and candlelight in luxuriant bedouin tents, we can't help feeling that Boris has found what he wants. Yet the more he struggles to find happiness outside himself, the more he is torn by what he left behind. Finally, after much soul-searching, he goes back to his monastery. For him, at least, not even Marlene Dietrich can compete with the promise of the interior life.

Even the scriptwriter didn't seem to find this convincing. But I thought it made a good metaphor. Movies themselves are rather like a desert escape. For a couple of hours we can forget ourselves in someone else's fantasy, as untouched by reality as Marlene Dietrich's hair in the desert wind. And, like Boris, we are looking outside for something we can only find within.

I call this the "media mirage," for the entertainment industries have engulfed us in a dream-within-a-dream world that promises to entertain and distract us every hour of the waking day. We have so much to choose from, but very little that is nourishing – and some that is directly harmful. In this sense, experience can be very much like junk food for the mind.

Most of us take nutrition for granted. We forget that just three or four generations ago, it was preposterous to think that disease could arise from the *lack* of something. But today, thanks more to advertisers than to public health efforts, everyone knows that the human body cannot grow strong without specific nutrients. We

STORY

Cutting the Cable

"Two years ago I moved to a new apartment, and because I thought my teenage son was spending too much time watching TV, I didn't get cable hooked up.

"He no longer misses it and I find it a great relief not to have it available. I no longer have the temptation to watch whatever is on, and consequently have more time to spend with my son and daughter, walk with the mantram, or read. Eliminating TV has made my life very much lighter and cleared out some mind pollution too."

– Helen T., New York

may not know exactly what folic acid is or why we need metals like zinc and iron in our tissues, but we accept that substances like these are necessary for good health.

It is the same with the mind. Like the body, the mind too can get tense and sick. It too needs relaxation, needs to be stretched and exercised. But most important – and almost unknown today – it needs to be nourished. It has its own minimum daily requirements for health and strength, and it grows weak – even ill – if it is deprived of them for too long.

You know the slogan "You are what you eat." I would say, "No, your body is what you eat. *You* are what you think." Just as the body is made of food, the mind is made of thoughts: everything we think, feel, and take in through the five senses.

> We need nourishing thoughts and experiences to make our minds strong.

All of us want food that is nourishing. I don't think anyone really wants to live on products that weaken the body, even if they look attractive and have a shelf life of ten years. Similarly, the mind needs nourishing thoughts – tenderness, kindness, compassion, good will. It needs experiences that will make it stronger, finer, more flexible. Everything the mind takes in becomes part of character and consciousness, and the sum of all that is who we are.

Bones and muscles seem so solid; thoughts and perceptions appear to leave no more impression than writing on water. But the contents of consciousness – the accumulation of everything we have thought, felt, perceived, and experienced – is much more long-lasting than bodily tissues. Proteins and cells are constantly being replaced, but what goes into the mind settles into the unconscious and stays there.

A doughnut may not linger in the stomach, but what the body makes of it can stay with us far too long – usually in the wrong places. Similarly, though experiences are transient, what the mind makes of them becomes part of us for the rest of our lives.

Doughnuts, of course, like to settle about the hips. Sense impressions settle in what the Buddha calls "storehouse consciousness." Just as a basement accumulates the stuff of a lifetime – forgotten photographs, discarded toys, brittle copies of *National Geographic* – the mind accumulates experiences in the basement of the unconscious.

And this accumulation is who we are. That is why, though physical nutrition is important, nothing is more vital than what we feed the mind. After all, we consume food only part of the day. The mind eats all day long.

Once we grasp this, we see that every day is a binge. If we're not careful, the result is like what happens when we go on eating junk food. Imagine eating nothing but french fries. You would become a potato person: Ms. Deepfry, Mr. Chips. You would look and feel terrible. It is the same with the mind. Stuffing ourselves through the senses bloats the personality, filling it with images and "sound bites."

It is absolutely crucial, therefore, to have some choice in what goes into our consciousness. Just as there is junk food for the body, there is junk food for the mind. And that brings us to the mass media, for today most of what the mind gets to eat is prepared and served by the entertainment industry.

I once went with a friend to see what we thought was a harmless comedy. It turned out to be savage and violent, with attempts at humor that I found degrading. When we leave the theater after an experience like this, I think most of us feel a little worse inside. Shows like this are at the expense of the mind, certainly not for its benefit.

Besides violence, of course, the other staple of the media is sex. In the movies, whenever the plot begins to wear thin, people start taking off their clothes.

At such times it is a study to watch the audience. Everybody – old, young, male, female – immediately gets absorbed. Even the popcorn is forgotten. That is not free concentration. It is compulsive, which is just as oppressive as compulsive eating.

Sooner or later, one way or another, what we assimilate this way begins to show in our behavior. I don't mean that we literally go out and imitate what we see on the screen, the way children often do. The real effects go deeper: we become more and more like the examples we choose to see.

In most of us, for example, incessant exposure to violence in the media doesn't build up until we erupt in mayhem. Instead, there is a gradual shift in character. Over time, we find we have developed a more belligerent attitude, aggressive language, abusive behavior, increasingly frequent urges to strike back at someone who cuts in front of us on the road. Even if we do not want to behave this way, it seems to surge up from deep within, unbidden. It is not so much specific actions we absorb as attitudes, language, and primal drives like anger, greed, and fear.

> The unconscious mind does not distinguish between "real" and "unreal." Everything is experience – and it all sinks in.

How can we nourish the mind (and still have some fun)?

We all need to unwind. The trouble is, the entertainment offered by the mass media is so often unhealthy. But what if you really feel like watching TV? Or your partner wants a night out at the movies? The key is to select really carefully. For instance, choose:

- *A drama that shows high ideals – people striving to be noble, strong, selfless, courageous – something that leaves you feeling inspired*
- *A comedy with harmless humor – it may not be great art, but laughter (if it's not at others' expense) is good for us, and you can take the children too*
- *A high-quality documentary – on nature, art, music, history, dance – whatever interests you, as long as it's uplifting*
- *A "feel-good" movie that's basically kind – something where the characters genuinely care about each other*

I can assure you that knowing the difference between film and reality does not make us immune to media experience. The unconscious draws no distinction between "real" and "unreal." Everything we take in through the senses is experience. Watching a thousand scenes of violence on the screen has much the same effect as in real life: it deadens sensitivity.

This is what the mass media can gradually do to us, and not only at viewing times. Our very instrument of enjoyment – the

Any of these, depending on your taste, can give you a break at home or a good evening out.

- *Volunteering*
- *Going to a concert, an art gallery, or an exhibition*

What else can you do to relax?

Simple things, such as:

- *Preparing and eating a meal with friends*
- *Gardening*
- *Making music, acting, painting*
- *Team sports, hiking in nature*

Try to find activities that you can do with others, so you share the benefits. Sometimes, of course, you may just want to relax on your own. But a strong social network protects you against stress and promotes harmony in the community. Good for you, good for everyone.

mind – is being dulled by degrees, and we take that lack of sensitivity into everything we do.

In such a state, what is it that we are absorbing? What image of ourselves is offered by the mass media, and how much of it do we want to assimilate?

Modern civilization tells us constantly that the human being is no more than the physical body. And of course that means that other people are physical objects too. This is perhaps the greatest superstition of our times. Everywhere I go I remind people, "You are not a biochemical product. You are a human being." I take very good care of my physical health, but my body is not me. It is the house in which I live. I am the resident; "Eknath Easwaran" is my address. Beneath all the shadow play of impurity and imperfection, aggression and hostility that we see around us, our real core

STORY

Habits Change

"I didn't realize until recently how much extraneous stuff I was doing, instead of focusing on things I truly enjoy that are beneficial to me. Like I used to join friends for a night on the town to listen to the blues. There are some good clubs around, and I love jazz guitar. But when I went out, I came home late and couldn't get up in the morning. My two days off were wasted because I was recovering.

"These days I still enjoy listening to music, but after I realized the negative effect it was having on me, going out to nightclubs was one of those things that just dropped away as if it never really mattered."

– Darlene L., Louisiana

is spirit: loving, forgiving, forbearing, tender, wise. This "original goodness" is what defines a human being.

> A healthy mind is all about choices. With any experience we should ask ourselves, "Will this make me calmer, wiser?"

Nutritionists remind us that before we eat something, we should ask, "Do I want this to be part of my body?" Similarly, we should remind ourselves every time we go out for entertainment or switch on the TV, "This experience is going to become part of me. Will I be the better for it? Will it leave me calmer, or will it agitate me? Will it make me more compassionate, or will it stir up anger or leave me depressed?"

In other words, I am talking about learning to make choices – reclaiming the power to choose what goes into your mind. After all, don't you like to choose the food you eat? It is the same with what you feed your mind.

When we start looking at everything like this, monotony goes out of life. Making these choices wisely throughout the day brings a deep integration of character, conduct, and consciousness.

The better you get to know your mind, the more you realize that this is not just a question of the media. The mind absorbs everything around it – everything it takes in.

Granny tried to teach me this right from childhood, though it took me half a lifetime to understand. Every year when school began, I would run home after the first day to tell her who I had played with and what we had done. "You don't have to tell me who you have been with," she would say. "I can tell."

"All right, Granny, who?"

She would proceed to name every one of them. And she was always right. "Granny," I would ask in amazement, "how did you know?"

And she would reply with an old saying that was often on her lips: "We become like those we associate with."

Granny wasn't one to waste words, so she never explained. It was only after I learned to meditate that I began to understand what she was trying to tell me. It wasn't simply a matter of imitating others' words or behavior. Granny was talking about the formation of character: how we absorb the influences around us, which shape the kind of person we are becoming for better or for worse.

We automatically absorb the influence of those around us – for better or worse.

In India this is often illustrated by comparing the mind to a crystal, which takes on the color of whatever is around it. Granny's explanation was more earthy: she compared the mind to a white cloth, which takes the color of everything it is dipped in. Even as a boy, I found this a sobering comparison. After being dipped a few times in a variety of experiences, the mind can really need a bath.

"We become like those we associate with." Behind that old saying lies an ancient bit of wisdom. What is good in us and what is bad, our strong points and our weak points alike, develop because of constant association with everything and everyone around us. When we associate with calm people, we become calmer; when we associate with agitated people, we become agitated. When we frequent the company of people who are wise, we become wiser; when our company is otherwise, we become otherwise too.

All of us have experienced this. When we spend an afternoon with a friend who is wrought up over some political issue or some gross injustice that has been done to him personally, we come home so agitated ourselves that we cannot sit and enjoy our dinner; we cannot sleep in peace. There may be no apparent connection with the other person's grievances; our mind is simply stirred up, racing at top speed. And we just can't understand: in the afternoon we were feeling so calm, so composed; what happened to get us so agitated? Then we remember: "Oh, yeah, we met Bob for coffee!"

The more intimate the relationship, of course, the more susceptible to this we are. When you go out with your boyfriend and come back agitated, I wouldn't call that person a boyfriend. The correct word is "boyfoe." When you go out with a girl who makes you agitated, she's not a girlfriend; she's a girlfoe. If we spend much time with people who talk negatively about themselves or others, for example, we begin to absorb these qualities and attitudes ourselves, no matter how immune we may feel – especially when we are vague about our own standards and values.

The reason for this is simple: we participate in other people's states of mind. This is not so far-fetched as it sounds. Because we

STORY

Anguish over Arguments

"My parents began arguing about ten years ago and it seems they've not stopped since. Once my father retired, they were with each other constantly and constantly getting on one another's nerves. My father slung harsh verbal abuse (actually calling her 'stupid'), while my mother interrupted him and contradicted him whenever she could get a word in edgewise.

"As you can imagine, being with them was extremely difficult – the atmosphere seemed literally toxic. Plus, as one of three daughters living nearby in a fairly close-knit family, it wasn't possible for me to avoid them, nor did I want to. Though they were so hard on one another, they were absolutely kind and caring to us and to their friends . . . It was very, very painful to watch these two people, whom I loved so much, constantly attack one another.

"Initially I tried the direct approach, asking them to please stop criticizing one another. Nothing changed, so I then explained how much they were hurting me by hurting one another. Again, nothing changed and I found myself full of anxiety before, during and after each visit with them. So, I decided to say my mantram and even write it out before each visit. I both 'sent' the mantram to them and directed it inward, so that at least I could stay calm even if they didn't.

"This helped immensely, I think, to protect myself from the pain, and I hope it did something to protect them. In the end, unfortunately, they separated – also a painful experience – and now I say my mantram for them for different reasons. But I will always remember how saying the mantram eased my anxiety during those difficult years. It's been a remarkable lesson for me in how we cannot 'fix' other people – only ourselves."

– Siobhan C., Ireland

are physically oriented, we think states of mind must be separate just as our bodies are. But thoughts have no containers. Consciousness is a kind of mental atmosphere: mental states commingle like the air we breathe. If one person in a room has the flu, others are likely to catch it in the air. Similarly, if one person in a home or office is angry, fearful, or depressed, that state of mind will spread to those around – and they will spread it to others.

Everyone has observed this in daily life. This kind of contagion is so common today that mental agitation – anger, negativity, hostility, greed – has become epidemic. Agitated people will always make a beeline for each other; and where two agitated people come together, the result can be explosive. Even one agitated person is enough to disturb the whole home, the whole office, even the whole community.

Speech is an important element in this contagion because the way people speak communicates their states of mind. For that reason, we need to be vigilant about the kind of conversation we participate in. One of the first things I learned from Granny's example was never to listen to gossip and never to repeat anything at another person's expense. In our home, whenever the conversation turned to what a particular neighbor had just done and why, she would say, "Come on, son, let's go out to the veranda." Everyone can do this: just excuse yourself politely and slip out. It's a helpful reminder all around.

Books, magazines, papers, movies, television, conversation – all these are part of the mental atmosphere we live in. To live in freedom, we have to ask ourselves constantly whether this is the kind of air we want to breathe, for these are powerful influences on the kind of person we are becoming every day.

Even our thoughts are part of this atmosphere. Negative thoughts are the worst kind of company because it is so difficult to throw them out. That is why I advise that whenever you find yourself caught in negative thinking, start repeating the mantram. When the mind is absorbed in the mantram, it has no room for other thoughts. It is alert, calm, and focused always.

> We become stronger, nobler, more secure by association – by spending time with those who embody the qualities that we admire.

Desire for positive company comes naturally once we decide we want to improve ourselves. As we begin to change inside, some of our tastes and even friendships may change too. It's normal to start looking for the company of others who will strengthen the qualities we are trying to develop in ourselves.

This is the positive side of the power of association: we absorb good qualities, too, by spending time with people who embody them. If you want to be secure and generous, the Buddha says, associate with people who are secure and generous. Learn to be like them in their daily example. By association we can become good; by association we can become strong; by association we can elevate ourselves to a nobler way of life.

You may have experienced this as well. When you are agitated about something and want to express it by agitating others, you go by mistake to the house of someone who is calm and secure. He comes to the door, sees the turmoil in your eyes, and says, "Come on in! You can leave your mind in overdrive and race along however you like." You start recapitulating what wrongs the world has done you, how you have always been innocent, and your friend just sits and listens. Halfway you begin to say, "Maybe sometimes I do make mistakes. Maybe sometimes I do provoke people myself."

Your friend is still not saying anything. He is just listening with love and understanding. But by the time your visit ends, you find you have calmed down. And you just don't know what has happened to your agitation. It takes most of us a long time to understand: "We become like those we associate with." We participate in their mental states – in this case for the better.

Personally, I take this even farther. We all need human companionship, but we need transcendent companionship too. The highest form of spiritual association is with those who embody our highest ideals and aspirations, who remind us of what we want to be like in every way we can. It might be Jesus or the Compassionate Buddha; it might be a great saint or other beacon figure like Mahatma Gandhi, Francis of Assisi, Teresa of Avila, or Thérèse of Lisieux.

And this does not require a physical presence. These figures are not dead. They continue to guide us. Their bodies are gone, but their influences move about freely in the world, helping those who respond with a unified heart. Luminous figures like these can be living companions. By reading about them, thinking about them, meditating on their words, we can bring their presence into our daily lives.

But the deepest nourishment comes from within. When the mind is still, it absorbs strength from an inner source that is not personal but universal.

I said earlier that the mind needs nourishing thoughts, like kindness and good will. This is something to reflect on. Everyone desires kindness, but what we really need is to *be* kind. Everyone wants to be loved, but our real need is to love. Everyone seeks gratitude, respect, understanding; we feel starved when we're treated otherwise. But what actually starves us is not showing gratitude, respect, and understanding to others. This is the surest sign I know of that all of us are one: by giving to those around us, we nourish ourselves as well.

KEY IDEAS

Chapter Four: Nourish Your Mind

1. We need nourishing thoughts and experiences to make our minds strong.

2. The unconscious mind does not distinguish between "real" and "unreal." Everything is experience – and it all sinks in.

3. We should choose carefully what goes into our consciousness – particularly with the mass media.

4. A healthy mind is all about choices. We should frequently ask ourselves, "Will this make me calmer, wiser?"

5. We automatically absorb the influence of those around us – for better or worse.

6. We become stronger and more secure by association – by spending time with those who embody the qualities that we admire.

POINTS TO PRACTICE

Nourishing the Mind

1. Plan a "nourishing outing" with friends or family. Choose an activity that relaxes your mind, nourishes your spirit, and cheers your heart. (See the sidebar on pages 92–93 for a few ideas.)

2. Here is a week-long experiment in substituting uplifting stuff for not-so-uplifting stuff.

The first part of your task is to find some uplifting activities: a favorite book or movie, good music, whatever, so long as it is something that leaves you feeling refreshed and renewed.

Then, for one week, use the time that you would normally spend on TV or other less-than-uplifting activities to immerse yourself in the more positive ones you've chosen.

At the end of the week, see if you notice any changes in your mental atmosphere.

3. Is there someone in your life whose agitation rubs off on you? Try this experiment. Before spending time with this person, repeat your mantram – or, even better, take a brisk mantram walk (as described at the end of page 79). Then, while you are with the person, do your best to remain calm and not add to the agitated atmosphere.

Later, evaluate the experiment. Were you a little less agitated than usual this time? Did it make any difference in the quality of the time you spent together?

4. Institute a Kind Words Day. For one whole day, choose your words carefully. Cultivate an attitude of cheerfulness. Do your best to find positive things to say in all circumstances.

At the end of the day, take a few quiet minutes to evaluate the experiment. Did it affect your own state of mind? Do you think it affected others' states of mind?

5. *Quiet as Nourishment:* In the very beginning of this chapter (pages 83–85), Christine describes how she and Easwaran nourished their minds with times of quiet. Does this description appeal to you, reminding you of how cool, clear water tastes to someone who's thirsty? If it does, plan a day of quiet. If you have friends with a similar thirst, get them to join in. Use Christine's suggestions to plan your day:

"Shut the door to the outside world . . . turn off the phone and TV and follow a quiet schedule together: mantram walks, reading, whatever nourishes your mind and lets you remember your real priorities."

INSPIRATION

Radiant Is the World Soul

Radiant is the world soul,
Full of splendor and beauty,
Full of life,
Of souls hidden,
Of treasures of the holy spirit,
Of fountains of strength,
Of greatness and beauty.
Proudly I ascend
Toward the heights of the world soul
That gives life to the universe.
How majestic the vision,
Come, enjoy,
Come, find peace,
Embrace delight,
Taste and see that God is good.
Why spend your substance on what does not nourish
and your labor on what cannot satisfy?
Listen to me, and you will enjoy what is good,
And find delight in what is truly precious.

– ABRAHAM ISAAC KOOK

CHAPTER FIVE

Choose Kindness

When we get upset, it's not because life upsets us. We get upset because we're upsettable. With practice, everyone can develop a mind that's unupsettable. One of the best ways to do this is to give complete attention and respect to those around us – particularly when we differ.

The Power of Words

Introduction by Christine Easwaran

Listening to Easwaran was an adventure. Suddenly, in the midst of talking about something ordinary, he would make a startling observation that would give me an entirely new perspective.

In the next few pages, he brings in a favorite comment from the Buddha: we don't get upset because people upset us; we get upset because we're upsettable. Another "mechanical problem": the mind can learn to be *un*upsettable.

Yet the most important insight is what follows. All of us want people to treat us with kindness and respect. We get upset when they don't. To make ourselves unupsettable, Easwaran says, the secret is simple: treat *others* with the kindness and respect we want for ourselves. We can't change them, after all. If we want less friction, our only practical choice is to make changes in ourselves.

Does that mean we can expect people to treat us with kindness when we do this? No, though I think they're much more likely to. What Easwaran is saying is that when we speak and act with kindness, we make ourselves so secure that others' unkindness doesn't shake us.

Easwaran chose his words carefully. At first I thought this might be because English was not his mother tongue, or that his legal training made him cautious, or perhaps because his field was literature and he loved beautiful language. With a little reflection, I realized there was a more important reason.

Words are things, Easwaran tells us in this chapter. They have consequences, sometimes elevating, sometimes destructive. They can hurt, heal, or inspire; inform, confuse, or deceive. They can restore a life or ruin one. And they can divide as easily as they can unite. Words can build bridges, but they can also wall others out.

This can happen at a very early age, even between parent and child. Such barriers come in the way again later in life, particularly when roles are reversed and an adult child has to assume the care of an aging parent. One good friend described this recently:

> *Five years ago, after my mother and I had been estranged for many years, she was severely injured in an accident. As her finances became depleted and her needs for care increased, we determined it would be best to have Mom move into our home. I was very fearful at first about having her live in my home. Because of past verbal and emotional abuse, I had little trust or respect for her, and although I was able to be pleasant and empathize with her daily difficulties, I really did not welcome the idea of having to cope with her all day every day. I had to learn to deal with much less privacy and consistent intrusions when I wanted time alone . . .*

It seems common for childhood wounds to flare up again in circumstances like this. Yet opportunities sometimes hide in such situations. Easwaran often reminded us that our own children will learn from how we treat our parents – and even if you don't have children watching, you will find that your own acts of kindness can actually heal old wounds. That's what happened in this instance; another friend tells a similar story on page 128.

I have noticed that Easwaran followed three principles in his own speech: be kind, be positive, be intentional. Words out of control can hurt badly; kind words and self-control can heal. Easwaran liked to quote a great medieval mystic, Ruysbroeck, who was asked for the secret of leading a spiritual life. Ruysbroeck replied, "Be kind. Be kind. Be kind."

If this sounds simplistic, try it. You will find that the effort to choose a kind response in the face of provocation reaches into the deepest recesses of consciousness.

To Easwaran, Ruysbroeck's advice was a plea for kindness on three levels: action, speech, and ultimately thought. Today, even to act with kindness consistently is a challenge: we're too speeded up to notice how others are affected by what we do. To be kind even in our thoughts sounds impossible – worth striving for only because in reaching for it, Easwaran says, we "grow till our heads touch the stars."

Between thought and action is kind speech, the focus of this chapter. The effort to choose kind words in the teeth of provocation gradually makes us kinder in action and even thought. No matter how serious the situation, Easwaran assures us, we can learn to disagree without being disagreeable. And as we do, we find we are including others instead of excluding them – gradually building bridges in our lives and even beyond.

Society today offers us great challenges for practicing these skills. Kindness has all but disappeared in private and public life. Political figures and their supporters hurl accusations with little regard for truth or relevance. Abusive language is widely considered good communication. I have long been alarmed at the extent to which broadcast indecency is invading our homes. And all this is on top of the way we often treat each other at home, at work, and even at play.

Our speech has power. If we are careless in the words we choose – or even deliberately negative – we can set in motion damaging forces that are as threatening as a viral epidemic. Or we can add our voice to the harmony that underlies all life by choosing our words with care, honesty, and – above all – kindness.

Choose Kindness

By Eknath Easwaran

As a boy, growing up in a South Indian village, I learned to ride an elephant the way teenagers today learn to drive a car. In our part of India, elephants are loved and deeply respected. They work in our fields and forests much like draft horses in the West, and have for thousands of years. They are highly intelligent, sensitive, loyal creatures, and the bond between an elephant and its trainer, or mahout, goes as deep as any family tie.

Elephants are very gentle. If you offer one a peanut on the palm of your hand, it won't grab; it will take the nut delicately with the tip of its trunk without even touching your skin. But its physical prowess is legendary. It can pull up a tree by the root and swing it around with its trunk as if it were a toy. Every creature gives way to the elephant; it has no natural enemies.

All ancient armies had infantry and cavalry. But Indian armies had elephantry too, and they were mightiest of all. A trained elephant will not turn back from battle. It would rather die than run away. And when an elephant goes into battle, its strength and endurance are so tremendous that no matter how many arrows find their mark on its body, it ignores them and presses forward gallantly into the thick of the fight.

Why am I telling you about elephants? Because this is how we should go through life, the Buddha says. It's one of my favorite verses: "Suffer harsh words as an elephant suffers arrows on the battlefield. People are people, often ill-natured."

Unkind words can cause lasting wounds. People will hurt you – but you can choose not to hurt them back.

This is the authentic keynote of the Buddha. He doesn't pretend that everyone is divine, everyone an angel. He says, "Frankly speaking, most people lack courtesy. You can expect to be hurt. But you have a say in how much you are hurt – and how you are going to respond. Be like an elephant, the mightiest of creatures. Shrug off harsh words and move on."

Because words can't be seen, we throw them around without much consideration for their effect. But words are things. In fact, they are even more thinglike than material objects. If you are hit by a rock, the wound might take days to heal. But harsh words can cause a wound that festers for years, and the pain may last a lifetime.

Words leave lasting impressions. Dr. Wilder Penfield, the great Canadian neurosurgeon, described vividly the experiments that demonstrated how electric stimulation of the brain can revive experiences we thought were long forgotten. It's all still there, recorded deep in consciousness – emotional depth charges ready to explode when they are triggered.

Any little act or remark that fails the test of kindness – a joke, a wisecrack, thoughtless gossip, a judgmental opinion we pick up and pass on without consideration – can wreck a relationship, destroy trust, even cost a job. But the most glaring failure is the everyday quarrel. We just don't seem to know how to disagree without being disagreeable.

It starts simply enough: someone says something we disagree with, and for some reason we get angry. Or, of course, we say something they disagree with and *they* get angry. Either way, after just a few words, tempers fray and language starts deteriorating.

How many times have I heard even educated people begin an emotionally charged dialogue with the best of intentions: "We won't quarrel. Let us confine ourselves to the subject at hand." Within five minutes one is saying, "That's not what you told me last Saturday in front of the Wide World of Shoes!" And the other replies, "That wasn't in front of the Wide World of Shoes. It was the Narrow World of Shoes." Anything to quarrel, anything to contradict.

After that, the argument has nothing to do with the subject. It is mostly "You must have done this even as a child" and "I've heard stories about the way you behaved in high school." We may know we are being foolish, but by then we are caught; we can't escape. All of us have been in arguments like this.

Whenever I found myself caught in a foolish situation I used to ask my grandmother, "Granny, if you found yourself in a situation like this, what would you do?" It took years for me to understand her simple answer: "Son, I wouldn't get into a situation like that."

This is very practical advice. Don't get into quarrels in the first place. If you do find yourself getting caught in one, close your mouth, start your mantram, and take the closest exit. If you can, go for a fast walk – even five minutes will help to quiet your mind. You'll be surprised at how effective this is.

Be kind? Even when others are mean to me?

It can be tough. But it doesn't just help others – it helps you too. Here's how:

You are living up to your own high ideals. You want to be kind and patient, right? By not retaliating to rude or unkind behavior, you're being true to yourself.

You'll have a sense of peace. No more twinges of guilt – after a difficult family visit, for instance, where you managed to stay pleasant and loving. Whatever happens in the longer run, you'll know you did your best.

You're an example to others. No one likes family arguments or rows at work. If you can be patient, it helps others to work and live harmoniously too. That reduces stress for everybody, including you.

What about the times when I must make a stand?

Then you should do so – but prepare carefully. Be friendly and firm. Speak clearly, but show respect. It's hard, but it's the only way to get a message across – to a difficult colleague, for instance, or a

Even if somebody is being rude or unkind, it doesn't help to be unkind in return. It doesn't help the point you are trying to make, it doesn't help them, and it doesn't help you. The more unkind you are, the more angry the other person is going to be – and then the more angry *you* are going to be, until two people have ceased to be civilized human beings and have gone back to a previous stage of evolution.

If we could see what happens in the mind at times like these,

teen who stays out late. Here are the key steps:

Get some detachment from the situation. Never confront anyone when you're angry or afraid. Use the mantram and take time to calm down first.

Look at the needs of the whole group – in a family or a team, for instance. Work out what will benefit everyone best. This can help you face up to a difficult situation. Then you can decide what you need to say.

Stay slowed down. Allow plenty of time when you're talking with the other person. Your mind needs to be slowed down if you're to stay calm and kind.

Listen with attention. Listening shows respect and helps you pick up hidden problems – essential if you're to maintain a good, warm relationship and find an effective outcome.

Staying kind makes you strong. And the mantram doesn't just give you patience; it gives you courage too. With practice, you can become a powerful, loving support to all around you. Isn't that what we all want?

we would be embarrassed. The mind simply slips out of control, like a speeding car that careens all over the road. Only when we have some say in where our attention goes can we keep our hands on the wheel.

That is where the mantram can help. When you see your mind

STORY

Bold with Kindness

"I tend to feel hurt when I sense that a person dislikes me. I used to enact the same pattern: if I thought someone I liked did not like me, I would subconsciously fabricate reasons why I didn't like them and then give them the cold shoulder. Of course, that made any hope of being on friendly terms nearly impossible.

"One day I decided to practice what Easwaran said about kindness in the face of adversity. I had been trying to be friendly with the mother of a boy in Kathy's class at school, but she seemed to regard me only with contempt and disdain. This went on repeatedly for months while I swallowed my pride and greeted her over and over with kindness even though I felt hurt and at times angry that she seemed to me so unkind.

"Then one day, out of the blue, she spoke to me as if I were an old friend. After that we were always on friendly terms.

"I learned an important lesson that day. I may never know why a person says or acts the way they do, but by always treating them with kindness and respect, I leave the door open."

– Beth K., Minnesota

beginning to speed up, step on the brake and stop the words that are about to burst forth. If necessary, put your hand over your mouth – or bite your tongue; it won't hurt as much as words you'll regret later. When you are sure your mind is under control again – and only then! – you can reply with words that are kind, constructive, and respectful.

> The mantram brings an angry mind back under control, so that we can be more patient, more constructive.

If we were to ask the Buddha why we lose control at times like these, he would point out that the mind never was really in our control in the first place. The very nature of the mind is to be fickle, distractable, constantly in motion – in a word, to do whatever it likes. It can't bear not having its way. It can't bear to be contradicted, so we get angry and lash out with hurtful words. Most of us would be chagrined to see the underlying message: "You aren't worth my respect. My ideas are superior; you don't count."

To break this cycle, we have to reverse the process and learn to be patient under provocation. That's why the Buddha tells us to put up with hard words like an elephant shrugging off arrows. He's not being ancient India's answer to Ann Landers. He's a spiritual teacher, and he's telling us how to live in freedom instead of simply reacting to what others say and do. Shrug off the daily darts and arrows that life sends, he is telling us, but never shoot arrows at others. Never upset people with harsh words or actions.

Never be unkind to them or treat them with lack of respect, however they might behave themselves.

In other words, he is saying, we should be prepared for a certain amount of impoliteness and discourtesy in personal relationships, not because people are bad but because they can't control their minds – just like us.

One of the curious foibles of human nature is that we expect others to show courtesy to us, but we also expect them to bear with us if we happen to be a little rude now and then. We expect to have our way, but why should others have theirs? It's good, I think, not to get upset if you find somebody not showing respect to you, for the simple reason that you may well not be showing enough respect yourself.

Here the Buddha asks a simple question: "If you get displeased when others are unkind to you, why don't you get displeased when you are not kind to others?" There is no mystery about these things. You don't like anyone to be unkind to you. Why don't you remember that the other person is just like you? Like you, he doesn't like unkind words. Like you, she appreciates courtesy and respect.

Oddly enough, the person who usually gets upset is the man who expects extreme courtesy for himself, the woman who finds it easy to be discourteous to others. The realist says, "Well, the world is like that. It takes all sorts. Sometimes I let words slip that I regret. Why should I be surprised if it happens to others also?"

This simple shift in attitude can save us a lot of grief. The Buddha is not simply reminding us that people are going to upset us. We already knew that. He is saying that if we get upset, it's because we're upsettable. And the answer is to make ourselves unupsettable – which everyone can do with practice.

This is a remarkable point. Just think: you don't have to be upset in an upsetting situation! All of us have times when life doesn't bother us and other times when one wrong word sets us off like a volcano. What makes the difference? Only our state of mind – which we are learning to control.

This is the benefit of practicing kindness, and the implication is revolutionary. If we want not to be upset by rude words and unkind behavior, the answer is for *us* to be courteous and kind. It may not have an immediate effect on those around us, but with practice it becomes a shield so strong that other people's behavior will not bother us at all.

Believe me, for those of us who have had our intellects honed to be sarcastic, it's very difficult to keep from using sharp words. When you're being criticized or attacked, it's almost considered an intellectual responsibility to answer back with compound interest. And that's just what I used to do in faculty meetings, along with everyone else – until I began to understand that if somebody attacked me, there was no need to get angry. It didn't improve the situation on any level – and besides, something within me rebelled against being bounced around like a rubber ball. So I started repeating my mantram silently and keeping quiet.

It was not at all easy. Worse, it was misinterpreted. Somebody who used to keep quiet would think I was at a loss for an answer and join the others in jumping on me. It was difficult training, but very soon I began to see that I was getting detached – not from my colleagues, but from my own opinions. When they were criticizing my ideas, they weren't criticizing me. They were criticizing a statue they had sculpted and set up in the corner. Why should I be bothered if they threw darts at a statue they themselves had made?

This doesn't mean making a doormat of yourself. Just the opposite. It is training – learning to get your mind under control. The first goal is to break the connection between stimulus and response. Later, once you have a measure of detachment, you can reply to criticism without identifying yourself with your opinions or the other person with hers, choosing words that are kind, respectful, and to the point. The key is to have a choice.

The more insensitive the other person is, the more reason for

STORY

The Brother-in-law Test

"Another area in my life I really have to work at is relating to my brother-in-law. For some reason he really rubs me the wrong way, on a regular basis. I regularly rely on my mantram to prepare to be with him and I rely on my mantram when I'm with him also (to help me keep my mouth shut). This certainly brings me some peace, and it makes for a more peaceful environment for everyone else too.

"This is definitely a work in progress and requires consistent attention and work on my part. He's a real test for my practice."

– Jim H., Ontario

you to alert your mind to be calm and compassionate – and, if necessary, to face opposition firmly but tenderly. We aren't helping inconsiderate people when we give in to their demands or let them walk all over us. It only feeds the habit of rudeness to let them have their way. We have to learn to show respect by opposing them – tenderly, nonviolently, but firmly.

This is a lesson all of us need to learn, and it's not at all easy. Particularly in relationships where both parties are insecure, each will feel resentment but neither will say no because of fear that the other's affections may change. This is very common today, especially between parents and children. In such cases it is especially painful – and all the more necessary – to learn to oppose tenderly, with detachment and respect.

Criticism can be useful only when it is constructive. Comments can be useful only when they are friendly. Persuasion can be useful only when it is loving. Even from the point of effectiveness, then, unkind comments only add to the problem. Disrespectful criticism makes the situation worse.

> Criticism must be friendly and respectful if it's to work. Use the mantram first to get some detachment from the situation.

Often, of course, it is necessary to make a constructive comment or suggestion. It is the mental attitude – the tone, the respect, the genuine concern – with which we put forward ideas opposed to others' that makes the contribution effective.

STORY

Calmed by Kindness

To Sarah, an anesthesiologist, kindness seemed unrealistic in the operating room, where tensions can run high and everyone's under pressure. But she decided to give it a try.

"One morning just before an operation, the surgeon came in upset and angry. He slammed instruments around, criticized everything, and barked out orders. "I said, 'It seems like you are having a bad day. Is there anything I can do to help?' "He exclaimed sarcastically, 'Yes! You can get an IV in the baby on the third floor that nobody seems to be able to get an IV into.'

"Inserting an IV isn't the anesthesiologist's job, but I wanted to make an effort. 'Who is the little baby?' I asked. 'If this is what is frustrating you, I'll see if I can try.'

"He stopped what he was doing, put down his instruments, and looked at me. 'You'd do that for me?' he asked.

"'I can't go up to the floor,' I said, 'but why not have the nurse bring the baby to the recovery room and I'll do it as soon as I finish here.'

"Well, despite my best efforts, I wasn't able to get that IV in either. We both tried. But even though we were unsuccessful, his attitude was totally changed. He came and apologized to me later. He still had the problem, but I think he was grateful that somebody responded to his frustration.

"More interesting, the other staff in the room were so amazed that they all stood around with their mouths open. They saw an angry, controlling person absolutely change direction and say, 'I'm sorry I was in a bad mood.' They couldn't believe what they had heard.

"I wish it could be second nature for me to act this way. I still have trouble sometimes seeing where it fits, or how to make it fit. But I am more hopeful that it can work."

– Sarah V., Georgia

I would suggest that whenever you feel you have to make a suggestion opposed to someone else's, take time to get a little detached from the situation by repeating the mantram silently. Then, when your mind is calm, offer your suggestion in a friendly, warmhearted manner with genuine respect. This takes practice, but you will find that it works. It is effective.

Most personal disagreements, I would say, arise from the unwillingness to see the other person's point of view. It is not that we have to accept it, but under no circumstances should we refuse to acknowledge that the other person has a point of view – one that deserves to be listened to with respect and evaluated with detachment.

Most of us acknowledge this in principle, but in practice it is all too rare. It took years of retraining my mind to learn to listen with respect to opinions utterly opposed to mine, weigh them objectively, and either retain my own opinion or revise or throw it out according to what I learned.

When we are able to do this – to be completely loyal to our own ideals while respecting the integrity of those who differ from us – often they begin to respond. What matters is the friendliness we show, the attention with which we listen – and, more than anything else, the complete absence of any sense of superiority. The superiority complex is most rampant where our sense of separateness is inflamed. The less separate we feel from those around us, the less superior we will feel too.

Disagreements are great opportunities for spiritual growth. Learn to make yourself unshakable.

Once we grasp this, every disagreement becomes an opportunity for spiritual growth.

While I was teaching literature, I had a colleague whose manner and opinions were opposed to mine in every conceivable way. I probably worked on that relationship throughout my tenure on campus. Not only did I learn to stay calm when he attacked me; I went out of my way to be kind to him. I don't think the effort ever made much difference to him. Our relationship never changed: I never did succeed in winning him over.

But that didn't matter. What was thrilling to discover was how much I had grown by trying. Because of that challenge, I learned to make myself unshakable in any storm of criticism or ill will. That skill proved invaluable later, and those years of trial gave me one of the most important lessons I have ever learned in personal relationships.

Facing anger in particular – your own or others' – is one of life's best opportunities for training. It's very much like learning to lift weights. You start by lifting chairs, then tables, then a desk, and after a while you're lifting a VW Bug. You can pick up a thousand pounds like one of those Russian weight lifters, raise it over your head – "clean and jerk" – and then drop it onto the mat with a lot of noise.

It is the same with anger. You start with those absurd little quarrels about the Wide World of Shoes. As you learn to be patient, you get confidence. Next time, when a bigger outburst comes, instead of retaliating, being unkind, or making sarcastic remarks, you use the incident to train the muscles of your patience by repeating the mantram.

Just as we admire people who can lift a thousand pounds, we all benefit by being with somebody who can be patient under attack, kind when opposed, and detached enough to see the situation clearly and compassionately. This is not a sign of weakness; it's a sign of immense strength. (Remember the Buddha and his elephant?)

Athletes, I understand, often keep a daily record of their training. In the same spirit, I take a few minutes every evening to get a bird's-eye view of training my mind and see where I can improve the quality of my daily behavior.

This is not a negative survey. You are not finding fault with yourself. You are asking, "Where can I be a little more patient? Can I be a little more loving toward Amelia tomorrow? Can I be a little more helpful to John?" These are positive ways in which we can improve the quality of our daily living tomorrow in the light of what we have done today.

Interestingly enough, this makes every day new. Tomorrow is never the same old day. There is always something more to be done: one or two more steps to take on the path upward, some greater care to avoid the mistakes that all of us make in some

STORY

Bringing Home the Challenge

After years of verbal abuse in her childhood, Eileen was worried that she might not be able to share her house with her mother, let alone be her caregiver. Patience and the mantram, she discovered, have limitless power to heal even lifelong wounds.

"The first month or two was a major adjustment, with constant friction and occasional bursts of toxic verbal abuse. I just used my mantram constantly (even if a bit grimly at times) and asked God for help.

"To my surprise, both my mom and I were able to cope. I actually found that having her live with us helped me to understand her much better, which in turn made me feel better. I have developed more compassion and understanding for her plight, more patience to cope with her temper and stubbornness. I see the benefits to Mom also, for her health is better and she is far less anxious and irritable.

"When we find someone difficult, Easwaran says, we should try writing down all the positives we can think of about that person. That was a real eye-opener! I was amazed that I could come up with a very long list of my mother's wonderful qualities and accomplishments.

"Since then life with Mom has been much more enjoyable. I find I have developed a stronger appreciation for her and a sense of humor about her idiosyncrasies. I believe that all my relationships have benefited from my increased generosity of spirit toward her.

"Today, I actually can't imagine life without Mom greeting my husband and me each morning and giving us the latest update on the weather and news. We have come to rely on it!"

– Eileen S., Idaho

small way. Instead of repining over mistakes or being resentful over them, I would suggest taking every possible care not to repeat those mistakes tomorrow and make at least a little improvement in your daily behavior.

This is why we have been given the competitive instinct: not to compete with others, but to compete with ourselves. Every evening you can look at yourself in the mirror and say, "You did a pretty good job today, I agree. But watch out! Tomorrow I'm going to outdo you."

When you refrain from unkindness, you are uncovering your real nature. Unkindness is not really characteristic of anyone. Beneath the selfish conditioning that brings such sorrow to us and others is a core of goodness that is an essential part of the human personality. The behavior that covers this goodness is a mask, which we gradually remove in the natural course of spiritual growth. We don't have to make ourselves loving; we have only to remove unkindness from our speech and finally from our hearts.

> If we can be kind when others provoke us,
> we move in the world with true freedom.

Those who have learned to be kind in the face of provocation move in the world with freedom. Their love flows to all around without any question of "Is he being nice to me? Is she being kind?" Life holds us hostage with such questions. But when we attain the stage where there is no possibility of my dancing to your tune or making you dance to mine, we are free. Life cannot dictate to us; we can choose how we respond.

KEY IDEAS

Chapter Five: Choose Kindness

1. Unkind words can cause lasting wounds. People will hurt you – but you can choose not to hurt them back.

2. The mantram brings an angry mind back under control, so we can be more patient, more constructive.

3. Criticism must be friendly and respectful if it's to work. Use the mantram to get some detachment from the situation.

4. Disagreements are great opportunities for spiritual growth. Learn to make yourself unshakable.

5. If we can be kind when others provoke us, we move in the world with true freedom.

POINTS TO PRACTICE

Choose Kindness

1. Do you have a difficult person in your life? If you do – and if you're ready for a big challenge – you might try this exercise:

- Write down a list of all the person's good qualities, or the good things he or she has done in the past.
- Then make an effort to only speak kindly about this person to others. (Or at least don't speak unkindly.)
- Take a good, long mantram walk just before the next time you are scheduled to meet. (It's likely you will need another mantram walk afterwards, too!)

That evening, ask yourself:

- Was it pleasant? (No.)
- Did the person change? (Probably not.)
- Will the person change in the future? (Unlikely.)
- Can *I* change? In what way? (This is the real challenge.)

2. Here is a great way to practice becoming unupsettable. Sit down with a friend who has an opinion that's opposed to yours. (He's a Yankees fan and you would die for the Red Sox; you love country music and he's into opera . . .) Repeat your mantram a few times, take a deep breath, and ask something like, "Who do you think is the greatest tenor of all time?"

Then listen. Don't bother thinking up rebuttals. Try not to judge. Just listen with interest – and, if you can, actually smile.

Afterwards, if you need it, take a brisk mantram walk – and give yourself a pat on the back! Frequent exercises like this will make you amazingly unshakable (despite the risk of turning you into a Caruso fan).

3. Give up gossip? Never! Gossip has its fun side, after all. It gives friends something to do together, it's cheap, and it's endlessly entertaining.

There's only one downside – it's so negative that it can often be hurtful. Suppose you turn it inside out? Suppose you only pass on the *positive* things that people say about each other? With that little change, you can actually build bridges of good will – even during coffee breaks at the office.

Why not try it for three days? Spread only positive gossip.

4. Try this prescription for a low-down mean and nasty day. (Some days are just like that: you wake up grumpy and it just keeps getting worse.) Next time this happens, go on a kindness spree. Everywhere you go, do something nice for someone. Spread kind words and smiles like largesse. Pet the neighbor's dog, carry the groceries in for the harried mom across the street, give your bus seat to the tired man standing in the aisle. Even if at first it just seems an act, go on throwing kindness around and see what happens.

INSPIRATION

Twin Verses

Our life is shaped by our mind: we become what we think. Suffering follows an evil thought as the wheels of a cart follow the oxen that draw it. Our life is shaped by our mind: we become what we think. Joy follows a pure thought like a shadow that never leaves.

"He was angry with me, he attacked me, he defeated me, he robbed me" – those who dwell on such thoughts will never be free from hatred. "He was angry with me, he attacked me, he defeated me, he robbed me" – those who do not dwell on such thoughts will surely become free from hatred.

For hatred can never put an end to hatred; love alone can. This is an unalterable law.

People forget that their lives will end soon. For those who remember, quarrels come to an end.

– THE BUDDHA

CHAPTER SIX

Light the Darkness

A calm mind has great power. It generates calm around it – a field of peace in which anger, fear, and violence can subside. By learning to calm the mind, each of us can become an instrument of peace.

We Can All Be Heroes

Introduction by Christine Easwaran

On September 12, 2001, a friend in New York sent a note that touched me deeply:

> *Your messages are just what I need to hear. At a time when so many are responding with heroic efforts, people like me need to know what can be done on our part, because not everyone can be a hero. I see now that the best thing I can do is to continue to try to be a force for peace and good through meditation and the mantram.*

We can all be heroes in our own spheres. That is how I feel after reading the stories of friends like those in this book who have been applying Easwaran's teachings in their lives. All of them describe themselves as ordinary. I find each one extraordinary, whether it is a young child with a dangerous illness or a man facing surgery he knows he might not survive.

These people are using spiritual skills to face highly challenging situations. They aren't trying to change others; they are simply dealing with difficulties by changing themselves. In the process, however, they are making a lasting difference in the lives of those they live and work with. And these skills are not just for grown-ups. Even a child can use the power of the mantram to stay calm and resourceful in times of fear and crisis.

Easwaran has been talking about how we are affected by those around us. The same principle is at play in how we affect others. When we strengthen our own values and put them into practice in our daily lives, we exercise an influence that can spread without limit. Just how far can be seen in the life of Saint Francis of Assisi, whose example swept the breadth of Europe in his short lifetime and continues to change lives today, almost a thousand years later.

What kind of person do we want to be? What kind of world do we want to live in? As Easwaran assures us, each of us has the inner resources we need to help make a better world.

Although this is work for a lifetime, it is a spiritual law that as we grow, circumstances around us change to open up greater opportunities to make a contribution.

The resources you bring to this challenge will be your own. We belong to different faiths, different nationalities, different political persuasions and philosophies; the ways we choose to tackle problems will be as varied as our human family. What unites us is our humanity and a lofty legacy of spiritual ideals that all the world's great wisdom traditions share. On this common ground, each of us can make a contribution that is urgently needed today.

Recently we received a beautiful letter from a young friend, Naomi, who speaks eloquently of her own struggle with the negative forces within and around us all:

I was brought up in a pretty rough Brooklyn neighborhood where one learned how to survive by grabbing what one could before someone else got it and going to any lengths to protect it. If one didn't play the game of life that way, it seemed, one would lose the game. Now I see that this way of thinking only causes great pain for those who think that way and everyone around them.

As my spiritual practice deepened, I began to change inside. Oftentimes I am surprised and relieved by my reactions to life and my authentic joy these days! Gandhi said we should become the change we want to see in the world, and I see the world so differently now. Empathy, compassion, a full heart, and an intense desire to help has taken up much of the room that once housed fear, resentment, greed, and selfishness.

I am now back in school, working on my teaching credential. Fame and Fortune were once my driving forces. Now my sincere desire is to serve, and I trust that my ultimate joy lies therein. I understand now why Gandhi was willing to die for the principles he so fervently believed in. I only want to live in a world where they exist.

To bring about a better world, let us start with our own lives. Easwaran has given us the skills we need, and we can begin in so many ways wherever we are. It is my earnest wish that each of you will feel inspired to use them to bring strength and hope into your days, and through you to those you live and work with and love.

Light the Darkness

By Eknath Easwaran

For most people, I imagine, radio has lost its magic. But I remember vividly the awe I felt as a boy in my remote Indian village when I first heard, as if by magic, a box with knobs and dials pull out of the air a thin voice from thousands of miles away: "Good evening. This is the BBC . . ."

Today, of course, the air around us is awash with messages at different frequencies. Music, news, chatter, advertisements – we can tune to whatever we like.

It is very much the same with the mind. All of us know how sensitive we can be to feelings around us. We sense tension when we walk into a room, register the hostility in a meeting, vibrate with the emotions of a football crowd. And in times of crisis, when the very air seems full of fear and anger, everybody's internal radio picks up the mood – and, all too often, passes it on.

This is a useful illustration, because it reminds us that the mind can be tuned. We do not have to accept the fear or anger around us; we can tune to a more positive channel. And when we do this, we are not the only ones who benefit. Just as everyone in a café relaxes when loud music is turned off, not tuning in to anger creates a zone of calm that helps those nearby calm down too.

This is easiest to see by negative example. You must have noticed how easily one person's irritation is picked up by others. We bring it home and pass it around until everybody in the family falls asleep in it. Whenever we are discourteous, unkind, inconsiderate, selfish, we are broadcasting emotional states for others to pick up, even if we do not express our feelings in words or action. It's not the passing event it seems. The signal has been sent, and like sound or light, it goes on spreading.

STORY

Transforming Negative Reactions

"Here's an incident where I recall using the mantram to great effect. I went into the bank with a kind of fuzzy question. The teller responded in an impatient, rude way – I felt like I had 'idiot' written across my forehead. My usual response would be anger, or just to leave without the info I wanted. But I know that arguing leads to agitation and unkindness and fleeing leads to a different kind of unsettledness (probably further resentment). So I started silently repeating the mantram while at the counter, and asked for her help and patience in a kind but determined way.

"By my staying calm, the question got answered – and because I faced a difficult situation with less agitation, I felt great when I left! Plus, I didn't have an angry-thoughts hangover."

–Julia F., England

> We broadcast our emotional states – positive or negative – to others. And the signals go on spreading.

Similarly, when we are kind to somebody, a little force of kindness is released in the field of consciousness around us. If we go on being kind, the force becomes stronger. And when we do this every day, even to people who are unkind to us, the force becomes potent and reaches far. Even as you read this, such forces are at work within and around you. Kindness is working against unkindness, and the stronger it is, the farther it will reach.

This is crucial, for as Emerson says, "The ancestor of every action is a thought." How we think shapes how we act, and the net effect of how each of us thinks and feels shapes the behavior of the groups we live in. The family is affected; co-workers are affected; eventually there is an effect on society itself.

And just as personal interactions shape the dynamics of a home or office or community, the sum total of all these interactions shapes the events of history. Markets are moved by the fear and greed of millions. Collective fear and helplessness can put a dictator into power. Anger multiplied a million times erupts in violence and triggers wars: leaders arise who are attuned to those emotions and express them in destructive action.

The mental states we tune to actually gain strength from the attention we give them. The more attention we give, the stronger they become. And just as people become addicted to drugs, the mind can become addicted to certain kinds of thinking. Fear is a drug; it can alter consciousness. So can greed. Anger is one of the most powerful of drugs, far more addictive than cocaine.

Nothing is more important for the modern world to understand. Any decision or action taken under the influence of fear, anger, or greed *has* to be disastrous. That is why most international policies are not successful: they are taken under the influence of fear, greed, and anger.

> Negative states fade if they are not reinforced. Remove negativity, and what remains is our original goodness.

Fortunately, negative states of mind fade if they are not reinforced by repetition. However strong they appear, they come and go. What is positive in consciousness is permanent, unchanging. That is why I say that original goodness is part of our very nature. When we cease to feed negativity with our attention, what remains is positive. We can strengthen what is positive by removing negativity from our minds. That is what spiritual practices like the mantram can do.

The mind, then, is not only a receiver. It is also a repeater, passing on what it receives. Most of us have only a few watts to broadcast with, while someone like Gandhi could send his message around the world. But each of us is on the air. We broadcast what we are, and others pick it up. When Gandhi said "My life is my message," he was speaking for us all.

Most of us do not like the idea of being a passive repeater for other people's messages. We want to have a positive influence. Why do our lives seem to have so little effect?

The answer is that most of us have minds that are scattered or distracted: sometimes positive, sometimes negative, constantly changing with our shifting moods and desires. If we don't seem to have much effect on the world we live in, it's because the signals we broadcast are weak and confused. It is the concentrated, focused mind that reaches people. All the great changes in the world for good and for ill have come from the impact of men and women with an overriding singleness of purpose and a concentrated mind. In our own times, on the positive side, Gandhi is a perfect example.

Fortunately, none of us are stuck with the mind we're born with. With practice, a distracted mind can be made one-pointed. By skills like repeating the mantram and learning to focus on one thing at a time, the mind can be made one-pointed on the essential goodness in every human heart. Then every negative emotion can gradually be transformed into a force for good. Anger, the most destructive of emotions – destructive of health, of peace of mind, of relationships, of life itself – can, when transformed, become a loving force that can change the world.

We have been born to be of help to others.
To make our full contribution, we need to train
the mind to be one-pointed and at peace.

It has been said that anyone who wants a peaceful life has chosen the wrong time to be born. The last hundred years have seen incessant turbulence, change, and danger. Around the world, people are living with a deep anxiety about the future.

In such situations it is only natural to ask now and then, "Why was I born into times like these?" The answer I would give is that we have been born to be of help to others. Desperate times are a sign of a more desperate need. To make our full contribution, we

STORY

Receiving Violence, Sending Peace

"In 1998 I was a social worker in Oakland, and my work took place in the sketchiest part of town.

"One night I was walking home late when I was suddenly surrounded by five young guys. One of them took a swing at me, but I ducked, which only made him angrier. 'Merry Christmas!' he raged, swearing at me. Then he nailed me right in the face with his fist, breaking my nose, and blood streamed everywhere.

"But there was a split second in there, just before the blow, where I was able to look the youth in the eye and ask him not to do this. The mantram helped me to make this human connection and out loud I said: 'Please don't do this.'

"He still hit me, but after that one blow, they left. They could have easily kept at it – no one else was around to stop them. Repeating the mantram helped me stay calm enough to make eye contact and treat the young man with some measure of respect."

–Sherman C., Washington, D.C.

need to train the mind to be at peace and then radiate that peace to those around us.

Very few of us really know what peace of mind is, the phrase has become so hackneyed. To think peace of mind comes by using chemical aids or moving to a quiet cabin on the seashore is to deny the very understanding of the word *mind.* In order to have peace of mind, thinking should be under control rather than at the mercy of fear and anger.

I was never a very angry person, but as a boy I was known for my fear. My cousins and classmates were brave, but I was not. I would never get into a fight, not out of noble motives but out of fear.

I can tell quite a few stories here at my own expense. In our village there was a particular street I had to take in order to get to school each day. (In a village, you often can't just go around the block.) And on that street lived a number of much older boys whose goal in life was to terrify boys who were smaller. Every morning and every afternoon, they would be lounging around waiting for someone to taunt.

We didn't all draw their attention. Some of my cousins, who were small like me, loved nothing better than a good fight. They were never bothered. But I made an attractive target.

I have to say my tormentors could be creative. Even in those days, for example, my hair was rather sparse, and that provided material for all kinds of jokes and jibes. I would go down the street with my heart pounding and one of them would call out derisively, "Caw, caw!" and make signs with their hands like a crow's nest.

(A crow's nest is rather flimsy. If you look at one, you can see the crow inside.)

That really bothered me, so finally I went and told my mother. "Never mind them," she said. "You're a nice-looking boy. Why should you care what they call you?"

That didn't make me feel any better, so I went to my granny. "Son," she said, "there are two ways to deal with this. One is that I can help you deal with it yourself. The other is, I can do it for you."

"Granny," I said, "I like the second way better."

Granny was a woman of action and completely fearless. She went and told those boys something that almost made them leave town, and after that I never had trouble walking down that lane again.

Unfortunately, I couldn't take my granny to college. At age sixteen I began the long journey of learning how to deal with such problems on my own.

I took heart from the example of another fearful boy who had made himself fearless and showed all India how to throw off fear. By the time I went to college, Mahatma Gandhi had taken center stage in India, and he made his life an open book. Everyone in India knew that as a child he had been subject to all kinds of fears. Even as a young man, he confessed, he was afraid to go out at night without his wife.

And he was terrified of public speaking! Early in his law career he had to plead an open-and-shut case where all he had to say was, "Your honor, the accused owes my client fifty rupees and he won't pay." He stood up, opened his mouth, and couldn't get out a word.

Finally he had to hand the case over to a colleague and rush out of court humiliated.

That is the man who went to South Africa as a timid, untrained clerk and got drawn into selfless service. By the time he returned to India, twenty years later, all that fear had vanished. Against overwhelming odds and brutal opposition, he had led a completely nonviolent campaign against racial legislation in South Africa and won. In India, he could stand against the greatest empire the world had seen and say, "Do your worst. I will not retaliate, but I will never retreat."

> Through selfless service and the mantram,
> Gandhi changed his fear into fearlessness,
> anger into compassion, hatred into love.

Today we would ask, "What kind of therapy did he undergo? What workshops did he attend?" But Gandhi never set out to make himself fearless. He simply began trying to serve those around him, spending less and less time on indulging himself and more on helping others. And the primary skill he used to support himself in these efforts was repetition of the mantram. Effort and the mantram together changed fear into fearlessness, anger into compassion, hatred into love.

That transformation is the reason I consider Gandhi a beacon for our times. "I have learnt through bitter experience," he said, "the one supreme lesson to conserve my anger, and as heat conserved is transmuted into energy, even so our anger controlled can be transmuted into a power which can move the world." And he added, "I have not the slightest doubt that any man or woman can achieve what I have, if he or she would make the same effort and cultivate the same hope and faith." That is what the mantram can do.

To see how the mantram deals with fear, it helps to look again at the mechanics of the mind. Fear is a frantic flickering of attention: the mind is being whipped like a flame in the wind. Whatever the provocation, what handicaps us at such times is not so much an external threat as this inability to concentrate, this incapacity to hold our attention steady. And the practical application is that as attention becomes steady again, fear *has* to subside.

Flickering attention is a sure sign of a divided mind. Division is tension. Division is friction. Division is ineffectiveness. Division is futility. And a mind divided cannot stand. Most of us have a mind that is divided; that is why it sometimes cannot stand under the impact of life.

The mind can be compared to a huge highway with traffic racing along twenty-four hours a day. The problem is that thoughts don't know how to drive. They stop here and there, weave in and out of traffic, and race out of control, an utter danger to everyone around.

This is what most of us call thinking. And the practical problem is that if a thought creeps up alongside us in the next lane, we get distracted. It steals our attention. We see the license plate, FEAR, and we start trembling. We keep glancing over, get jittery, and abruptly find ourselves darting over into its lane. The next thing we know, Fear has a tow hook on our bumper and is dragging us wherever it likes.

This gives a practical clue to how to solve the problem of fear. If you learn to keep your attention steady, a negative emotion like fear can wave, honk, do anything it likes to distract you into its lane and get its tow hook on you; you won't react. Eventually it will have to go away, because you scarcely know it is there. Like a concentrated driver that cruises along smoothly in one lane, you cannot be distracted from your purpose.

Having a calm, steady mind is like driving a long distance in a powerful car on cruise control. You select the carpool lane and drive smoothly to your destination without any difficulty, danger, or delay – no compulsive darting into other people's lanes, no U-turns in the face of traffic, no being totaled and towed away.

And the mantram can help us get where we want to go. The mantram has the power to transform negative forces in the mind into positive ones. There is nothing magical about this; the mantram simply takes advantage of the fact that when the mind is in the grip of negative emotions like fear and anger, thoughts are always racing. In positive states like love and compassion, consciousness is calm. So whenever the mind starts to race in fear or anger, repeating the mantram simply touches the brake.

Whenever a negative emotion starts to rise – a wisp of anxiety or fear, a rush of anger – if you can immediately start repeating your mantram in your mind, that gives the mind something to

STORY

A Child Chases Fear with the Mantram

"We were at a concert when my seven-year-old son, Chris, became feverish. We took him home and called the doctor. He said, 'Just treat the fever.'

"That night the fever shot up to 104 or 105. Chris was throwing up violently and his head was killing him. In the morning we started to give him ice baths so he wouldn't have convulsions. Chris was using his mantram a lot; that was the only way he could get into the bathtub. His fever stayed at 104.

"Then we took him to the hospital – carrying him, he was so sick. He couldn't hold his head up and his neck was very painful. They gave him IV medication right away and tested his white cell count. It was huge, so they put him on some extremely strong antibiotics.

"The next morning the fever returned. This time they tested him for meningitis. He was positive.

"During the whole time the mantram really helped Chris. He thought he was going to die, he felt so bad. He said to me, 'Mom, am I going to die?' I was crying and I said, 'No, Chris, you're not going to die.' I just knew deep down that he wasn't going to die, but that he was very, very sick.

"He said to me, 'Mom, just say my mantram for me.' He was so sick he didn't even have the energy to talk, so I kept whispering in his ear. During all this he never complained. The nurses couldn't believe it. If I stopped saying the mantram, he would say, 'Keep saying it, Mom.' He didn't even get nervous when they were doing the spinal tap.

"Gradually he started to recover, though it took a couple of months before he really felt better. It showed me that in Chris's worst hour, he had somewhere to turn – the Holy Name – and it had great benefit for him and for us, his family." – Kim R., Holland

hold on to. If you can continue to hold on to the mantram at such times, the energy in that emotion is transformed, very much the way the energy of a rushing river is transformed into electricity. That is the secret of the mantram's power.

> Hold on to the mantram when fear or anger arises – it will steady your mind. Then you are free to respond to life's challenges as you choose.

Today, after years of practice, I can assure you on the basis of my own experience that when you are repeating the mantram with full attention, no fear can enter and oppress you. The mantram will be cruising the highways of consciousness like a traffic officer on a Harley Davidson. That is the surest way of preventing the mind from wandering into strange byways where nothing but what is unpleasant waits for us.

The mantram is particularly precious for children dealing with fear, because it is so simple it can be practiced at any age. The other day at the hospital, for example, I saw a small child being given an injection. The wailing wrung my heart. That's why I take every opportunity to tell mothers to teach their children to repeat the mantram at the earliest possible age. When they go to the dentist, when they feel threatened, when they hurt themselves or have nightmares, the mantram is of immense help.

In the depths of consciousness, even the bravest among us lives in a world of fear – the result of deep evolutionary conditioning that tells us we are separate and alone in a hostile world. We are protected from this awareness by a merciful amnesia that allows us to function outside the jungle, but deep in consciousness these fears are always present, manifesting themselves whenever we let our minds get agitated by events around us.

We could make a catalog of these fears, but they all stem from one fatal superstition: the belief that we are merely physical creatures, separate from the rest of life. A fragment cannot help feeling constantly alienated and alone, desperate for protection, always anxious that what it has will be taken away. Whatever face such people present to others and themselves, those who are acutely aware of their own separateness – their family, their community, their country, their race – are, beneath appearances, fragile and insecure. Their primary responses to life are to fight or to run away.

With the mantram, this sense of being separate and threatened by those around you gradually falls away. You will feel at home wherever you are, whoever you are with. You have a third alternative, beyond the conditioned reactions of fight and flight: the freedom to meet life's challenges with the response you choose.

In Indian mythology, the times we live in are called Kali Yuga, the "age of darkness." I call it the age of anger. With the world torn asunder by war and violence invading our cities and even our homes and schools, uncontrolled anger has become the hallmark of daily life. It saturates our media, our entertainment, our personal relationships, even our speech.

Over the years, I have witnessed a steady decline in the quality of life throughout the modern world as anger and violence become taken for granted as part of life. This is a trend that threatens everyone, for anger in one corner of the globe now can find expression thousands of miles away. With the technology of destruction within easy reach, one person full of hatred can wreak havoc and terror anywhere.

All of us harbor a good deal of anger; that is the human condition. But an angry person can never help lead an angry world from darkness into light – a responsibility that each of us needs to assume now if we want a safer world.

In the Truman Museum in Independence, Missouri, I saw an ancient clay lamp that had been presented to President Truman by the Jewish community of Boston. At its base was an inscription from Proverbs that is well known in English: "The spirit of man is the candle of the Lord."

Clay lamps like these are still common in village India. People pour in a little coconut oil, insert a wick, light it, and keep the lamp in the window on festival days. When the lamp is placed outside, the flame flickers wildly and may even go out if a breeze blows. But when the lamp is inside the home, in an alcove or shrine, the tongue of flame is absolutely still; it does not flicker at all.

> When the mind is still, we can become an instrument of peace.

That is how the mind should be: like the flame of a lamp in a windless place. It should not even flicker. When the mind does not flicker, there can be no fear. When the mind does not flicker, there can be no anger. All negative emotions are wild movements in the mind that vanish when the mind is still. In this state, we find the fulfillment of the wonderful prayer of Saint Francis: "Lord, make me an instrument of thy peace."

A calm mind releases the most precious capacity a human being can have: the capacity to turn anger into compassion, fear into fearlessness, and hatred into love. Ordinary people like you and me may not be a Gandhi or Saint Francis, but to the extent we can quiet our minds and light the lamp of wisdom within, we too can add a little light to the world around us instead of feeling helpless in the dark.

KEY IDEAS

Chapter Six: Light the Darkness

1. We broadcast our emotional states – positive or negative – to others. And the signals go on spreading.

2. Negative states of mind fade if they are not reinforced. Remove negativity, and what remains is our original goodness.

3. We have been born to be of help to others. To make our full contribution, we need to train the mind to be one-pointed and at peace.

4. Through selfless service and the mantram, Gandhi changed his fear into fearlessness, anger into compassion, hatred into love.

5. Hold on to the mantram when fear or anger arises – it will steady your mind.

6. When the mind is still, we can become an instrument of peace.

POINTS TO PRACTICE

Spreading Light

We live in such a speeded-up world that just getting through the day can take all we've got. But little gestures take little effort and can shift our focus to the larger world and others' needs.

1. Spread your blessings with your mantram. Try it for just one day. Everywhere you go, when you see strained faces or hear tension in a voice, when a siren howls or you feel sad about a piece of tragic news – use your mantram! Spread it silently far and wide. Let it light up the life, however briefly, of anyone who needs it, and imagine it leaving a glow of peace behind.

   Do this for a day. Write down your impressions that night.

2. Look around. Find little ways you can be of help. Wash the dishes for a tired roommate. Drive an elderly neighbor to her medical appointment. Watch your friend's kids so she can have a night out with her husband. Fill your day with innumerable hidden acts of kindness. You might not be thanked, and you might get tired or bored or both. If you do, repeat your mantram so you can keep doing it. (And don't forget to give yourself some healthy recreation too!)

3. Remember your To Be list (page 56)? Take it out and have a look at it again. Is there anything you want to change or add? Is there anything specific you could do *today* that has slipped your attention recently? Find a way to attend to it and put it on today's To Do list, top priority.

4. Have a "Spreading Light Party." Every group of friends, family, or colleagues has someone who's facing "stormy seas" - illness or crisis or heartbreak - and we wish there were something we could do to help. Get your group together. Bring pens and nice notepaper and spend an hour writing messages of love and support. Copy passages from inspiring books; include favorite pictures and a photo of yourselves. Pack it all up with some homemade cookies and send it off. It will arrive at your friend's door glowing like a little lamp of love.

5. At the end of each chapter of this book (pages 34, 58, 80, 106, 134, and 158) you've probably noticed an inspirational passage. Read these passages. Choose one that speaks to you about becoming "a lamp in a dark world" and memorize it. Write it out for yourself. Put it on your desk, by your phone, on the refrigerator, wherever you're likely to see it frequently. Let it remind you every day of the message it conveys and why you chose it.

INSPIRATION

Instrument of Peace

Lord, make me an instrument of thy peace.
Where there is hatred, let me sow love.
Where there is injury, pardon.
Where there is doubt, faith.
Where there is despair, hope.
Where there is darkness, light.
Where there is sadness, joy.

O divine Master, grant that I may not so much seek
To be consoled as to console,
To be understood as to understand,
To be loved as to love;
For it is in giving that we receive;
It is in pardoning that we are pardoned;
It is in dying to self that we are born to eternal life.

– THE PRAYER OF
SAINT FRANCIS OF ASSISI

AFTERWORD

Be an Island of Peace

By Christine Easwaran

In very few pages, Easwaran has covered a lot of ground. He began by giving us skills for coping with the challenges life throws at us. He assured us that we have everything we need within us to meet these challenges if we can learn how to keep our minds calm instead of panicky, angry, or despairing. That is the purpose of the tools he presents in the first three chapters: mantram repetition, slowing down, and one-pointed attention.

Then he goes on to suggest some unexpected ways to apply these skills. He reminds us that each of us needs kindness, yet what nourishes us is to give it. To keep from getting aggravated by other people, he advises *us* to listen with attention and reply with respect.

All this sounds backward – but it works. And as it works, something precious deep within us is released: something he calls our original goodness, hidden by the mind's agitation yet present in every one of us, simply by virtue of our being human.

So he ends by promising that in practicing these skills, we do much more than just help ourselves. Our personal example becomes an island of calm – at home, at work, wherever we go.

Our newfound peace of mind helps those around us stabilize their lives. These are forces, Easwaran tells us – goodness, kindness, generosity, love. Little by little, simply by trying, each of us can become a small force for peace.

Great teachers in every religion and every age have told us that goodness is as much a part of life as the force of gravity. The world would not endure for a single day without it. Somerset Maugham echoes this great truth in his enormously popular novel *The Razor's Edge,* published in 1943 in the midst of World War II. Referring to the story's main character, Maugham said, "Goodness is the strongest force in the world, and Larry has got it."

Larry is a young American whose experience of war prompts a long search for meaning. By the end of the novel, his life is completely changed; but he has no philosophy to teach, only the desire to lead an ordinary life ennobled by what he has learned. A friend challenges him: "Can you for a moment imagine that you, one man, can have any effect?"

"I can try," Larry replies. "Nothing that happens is without effect. If you throw a stone in a pond the universe isn't quite the same as it was before. . . . It may be that if I live the life I've planned for myself it may affect others; the effect may be no greater than the ripple caused by a stone thrown in a pond, but one ripple causes another, and that one a third; it's just possible that a few people will see that my way of life offers happiness and peace, and that they in turn will teach what they have learnt to others."

We should never underestimate the effect of one person remaining calm in the midst of turmoil, the power of one person to change ill will into good will, anger into compassion, hatred into love.

I do earnestly believe that the greatest danger that faces us today is fear and hatred. In words that belong to the whole world, the Prayer of Saint Francis (*see page 158*) tells how each of us can be a peacemaker in his or her own circle – an island for those around us, a force for peace, a shield against fear and anger.

You Are a Force for Peace

The first step is to bring calm to your own mind so you don't add fuel to the flames of fear and anger around you.

Keep this prayer in front of you. Put it on your desk. Don't let it become stale. Write it out. Memorize it. Repeat it to yourself whenever you feel overwhelmed. Give it to your friends. Keep it in your wallet. Teach it to your children. Recite it out loud. Put it on your refrigerator door.

You Are a Force for Peace

Don't get caught in angry, frightened talk. Choose what goes into your mind; don't leave it to the media. Don't let hostility and resentment take over your life. Step away from the whirlpools of negativity that swirl around us.

You Are a Force for Peace

Do something positive – every day. Take control of your life. Get together with your family and friends. Read elevating spiritual literature. Read with your children.

You Are a Force for Peace

Slow down. Stay focused. Pay attention to the needs of the people around you. Be kind and considerate. At home and at work, help create an atmosphere of trust and openness. Reach out to those you feel have offended you.

You Are a Force for Peace

Choose a mantram from the list on pages 32–33. Repeat it silently to yourself whenever you can – while washing the dishes, standing in line, waiting on hold. Repeat it whenever you start to get angry, upset, or afraid. Combine it often with a good, fast walk. Fall asleep repeating it so it stays with you throughout the night. Write it out by hand – fill a page or two with it every day. Write it for the whole world. Keep a little book for that purpose and carry it with you everywhere. The mind has to be working; give it the mantram.

You Are a Force for Peace

Teach your mantram to your children. Get them to repeat it whenever they can. Show them how powerful it can be by using it with them to keep calm. Tell them they too are a force for peace and the mantram can be their shield.

Keep reminding yourself that goodness is the strongest force in the world.

Further Resources

For more about the skills and ideas in this book, the Blue Mountain Center of Meditation, founded by Eknath Easwaran in 1961, offers books, programs, and audio and video materials. You'll find full instructions in Easwaran's Eight Point Program and passage meditation on our Web site, www.easwaran.org, as well as other resources for readers of Strength in the Storm.

The Eight Point Program

1. **Meditation on a Passage** Silent repetition in the mind of memorized inspirational passages from the world's great religions. Practiced for one-half hour each morning.

2. **Repetition of a Mantram** Silent repetition in the mind of a Holy Name or a hallowed phrase from one of the world's great religions. Practiced whenever possible throughout the day or night.

3. **Slowing Down** Setting priorities and reducing the stress and friction caused by hurry.

4. **One-Pointed Attention** Giving full concentration to the matter at hand.

5. **Training the Senses** Overcoming conditioned habits and learning to enjoy what is beneficial.

6. **Putting Others First** Gaining freedom from selfishness and separateness; finding joy in helping others.

7. **Spiritual Fellowship** Spending time regularly with others who are practicing passage meditation for mutual inspiration and support.

8. **Spiritual Reading** Drawing inspiration from writings by and about the world's great spiritual figures and from the scriptures of all religions. Studying Easwaran's works for general inspiration and for specific instruction in passage meditation.

The Eight Point Program

by Eknath Easwaran

These are the eight points of the program for a fuller, healthier, more spiritual life that I have used myself. They are explained and illustrated in my book *Passage Meditation,* which has a chapter on each point.

How to Meditate

The heart of this program is meditation. The principle of meditation is simple: we are what we think. When we meditate on inspired words with profound concentration, they have the capacity to sink into our consciousness, alive with a charge of spiritual awareness. Eventually these ideals become an integral part of our personality, which means they will find constant expression in what we do, what we say, and what we think.

Half an hour every morning, as early as is convenient, is the best time for meditation. Do not increase this period; if you want to meditate more, have half an hour in the evening also, preferably at the very end of the day.

Set aside a special place to be used only for meditation and spiritual reading. After a while that place will become associated with meditation in your mind, so that simply entering it will have a calming effect. If you cannot spare a room, have a particular corner. Whichever you choose, keep your meditation place clean, well ventilated, and reasonably austere.

Sit in a straight-backed chair or on the floor and gently close your eyes. If you sit on the floor, you may need to support your back lightly against a wall. You should be comfortable enough to forget your body, but not so comfortable that you become drowsy.

Whatever position you choose, be sure to keep your head, neck, and spinal column erect in a straight line. As concentration deepens, the nervous system relaxes and you may begin to fall asleep. It is important to resist this tendency right from the beginning by drawing yourself up and away from your back support until the wave of sleep has passed.

Once you have closed your eyes, begin to go slowly, in your mind, through one of the passages from the scriptures or the great mystics that I recommend for use in meditation. I usually suggest learning first the Prayer of Saint Francis of Assisi (*see page 158*). As you go through the prayer, let each word sink like a jewel into your consciousness.

In memorizing the prayer, it may be helpful to remind yourself that you are not addressing some being outside you. The kingdom of heaven is within us, and in this prayer we are calling deep into ourselves, appealing to the spark of the divine that is our real nature.

While you are meditating, do not follow any association of ideas or try to think about the passage. If you are giving your attention to each word, the meaning cannot help sinking in.

When distractions come, do not resist them, but give more attention to the words of the passage. If your mind strays from the passage entirely, bring it back gently to the beginning and start again.

When you reach the end of the passage, you may use it again as necessary to complete your period of meditation until you have memorized others. It is helpful to have a wide variety of passages for meditation, drawn from the world's major spiritual traditions. Each passage should be positive and practical, selected from a major scripture or a mystic of the highest stature. Many beautiful passages selected from the world's great spiritual traditions can be found in my collection *God Makes the Rivers to Flow.* Most of this book, too, is available on the Web: www.easwaran.org/passages.

When this Eight Point Program is followed daily to the best of one's ability, as I can testify from my own personal experience, it is possible for everyone to lead a secure, selfless life. Even a little such practice will begin to transform your life, leading to profoundly beneficial changes in yourself and the world around you.

Summary: Instructions in Meditation

- Choose a time for meditation when you can sit for half an hour in uninterrupted quiet. Early morning is best, before the activities of the day begin.
- Select a place that is cool, clean, and quiet.
- Sit with your back and head erect, on the floor or on a straight-backed chair. A back support may be helpful.
- Close your eyes and begin to go slowly, in your mind, through the words of a simple, positive inspirational passage from one of the world's great spiritual traditions.
- While meditating, do not follow any association of ideas or allow your mind to reflect on the meaning of the words. If you are giving your full attention to each word, the meaning cannot help sinking in.
- When distractions come, do not resist them, but give more attention to the words of the passage.
- When you reach the end of the passage, you may use it again as necessary to complete your period of meditation until you have memorized others.
- Resolve to have your meditation every day – however full your schedule, whatever interruptions threaten, whether you are sick or well.

Further Reading

If you've enjoyed *Strength in the Storm*, you may like to read other books by Easwaran. In this section you can find suggestions for further reading on the mantram, slowing down, inspirational passages, meditation, Gandhi and transforming anger, and understanding how the mind works and how to get it under control.

1. Would you like more on choosing and using a mantram?

Then read *The Mantram Handbook*. You'll find a detailed explanation of the meanings of many mantrams from the world's great spiritual traditions, but most of the book is about applying the mantram and using it to

- keep the mind steady
- overcome likes and dislikes
- deal with excitement and depression
- confront anger, fear, and greed
- stay calm at the time of death
- understand the goal of life

So you'll find more on some of the themes presented in *Strength in the Storm*, but you can also explore other areas of your life where the mantram will make all the difference in calming your mind.

2. Do you want more on slowing down and one-pointed attention?

Then *Take Your Time* would be a good choice. Its themes include finding balance in a hurried world, living in freedom, and taking time for relationships. This book has a particularly rich repertoire of stories and anecdotes to entertain us as well as inspire us to s-l-o-w down.

3. Did you enjoy the inspirational passages?

Then we have two suggestions for you.

God Makes the Rivers to Flow is a real treasure trove of nearly 150 inspirational passages from the world's great spiritual traditions. The passages in *Strength in the Storm* all come from *God Makes the Rivers to Flow.* There's an introduction by Eknath Easwaran, background notes on the passages, and a detailed section on how to use the book. "Slow, sustained concentration on these passages," says Easwaran, "drives them deep into our minds. And whatever we drive deep into our consciousness, that we become."

Words to Live By offers short daily readings based on quotations from outstanding spiritual figures, philosophers, and writers. Easwaran shows how we can apply these deep insights to our own lives. Read it in the morning to get your day off to a good start, or in the evening to calm the mind. "If we live right today," Easwaran assures us, "tomorrow has to be right."

Both these books are wonderful to dip into whenever you need nourishment for the mind.

4. Would you like to know more about Easwaran's method of passage meditation?

Then try *Passage Meditation: A Complete Spiritual Practice.* This book gives instructions in Easwaran's method of passage meditation, which is based on the concept that you are what you think. *Passage Meditation* gives you all the instructions and guidance you need, so you can get going right away in your own home.

Huston Smith, author of *The World's Religions,* wrote of *Passage Meditation:*

> *"No extravagant claims, no pretentious jargon.*
> *Just a clear, insightful exposition of meditation,*
> *and an excellent guide to its practice."*

5. Are you interested in more about Mahatma Gandhi?

Then you may like Easwaran's book *Gandhi the Man.* This book is different from the others in this section. It's the story of Gandhi's life and spiritual transformation, richly illustrated with photos. If you want to know more about transforming anger into compassion, then this book is for you.

Gandhi had a close follower who was a courageous and completely nonviolent Muslim leader, Khan Abdul Ghaffar Khan, later known as Badshah Khan. In his book *Nonviolent Soldier of Islam,* Easwaran tells the story of Badshah Khan's success with nonviolence in one of the most violent cultures in the modern world during India's struggle for independence. Few in the West have heard of Badshah Khan, but his life and work demonstrate the consistency between core Islamic principles and nonviolence.

> *"Eknath Easwaran's great achievement is telling an international audience about an Islamic practitioner of pacifism at a moment when few in the West understand its effectiveness and fewer still associate it with anything Islamic."* –The Washington Post

Like *Gandhi the Man, Nonviolent Soldier of Islam* includes some wonderful photos and is an absorbing and moving read.

6. Would you like to know more about training the mind?

One last suggestion: *Conquest of Mind* is Easwaran's guide to conscious living and the training of attention.

Conquest of Mind shows how we can choose the way we think – our feelings, our desires, the way we view the world and ourselves. Easwaran provides practical tools to enable us to control our minds and reshape our lives, using his Eight Point Program of daily meditation and supporting practices. You can find out more about breaking free from conditioned thinking processes, from brooding and worrying. And Easwaran gives a modern explanation of the Buddha's obstacles and opportunities in mastering the mind. It's an intriguing book if you want to know more about how your mind works – and how you can improve the way it functions.

Blue Mountain Center of Meditation

The Blue Mountain Center of Meditation publishes Eknath Easwaran's books, videos, and audio recordings, and offers retreats and online programs on passage meditation.

For more information and resources, please visit:

www.easwaran.org

The Blue Mountain Center of Meditation
Box 256, Tomales, California 94971

Telephone: + 1 707.878.2369
Toll-free in the US: 800.475.2369
Email: info@easwaran.org

Acknowledgments

We are grateful to the following translators and publishers for permission to reprint the following inspirational passages in this book:

p. 80 "The Mirror of This World," by Mahmud Shabestari, courtesy of the translator, Jonathan Star: from *The Inner Treasure: An Introduction to the World's Sacred and Mystical Writings,* tr. Jonathan Star (New York: J. P. Tarcher / Putnam), p. 137. Copyright 1999 by Jonathan Star.

p. 106 "Radiant Is the World Soul," by Rabbi Abraham Isaac Kook: Excerpt from *Abraham Isaac Kook: The Lights of Penitence, The Moral Principles, Lights of Holiness, Essays, Letters, and Poems,* translation and introduction by Ben Zion Bokser, from The Classics of Western Spirituality. Copyright ©1978 by Ben Zion Bokser, Paulist Press, Inc., New York/Mahwah, N.J. Used with permission of Paulist Press. www.paulistpress.com

Index